Published by Lexilore Publications
Printed in UK
ISBN 0-9550189-0-0

Lexilore Publications
Peveral Walk
Basingstoke
RG22 6QA

Acknowledgements

I would like to thank the following people for contributing to this book; Thanks must go to Tony Emmerson, Mark White, Barry Michael, David and Anthony Sullivan, for their appearance in some of the photographs shown. Christine Strachan for photography, Paul Flint and colleagues for helping me get the whole project off the ground. Especially the well respected and ultra strict Victor Kan (Sifu), for the intensive training and bitter/sweet memories over the six and a half years I learned from him. Also to my peers from the old school in London; Martin Bell, Kevin Gledhill, Jack Kontou, Michael Street, Pasco David, Arthur Caan. They are the unsung heroes of Wing Chun, all serving lengthy apprenticeships under Grandmaster Kan. Their depth of knowledge and "hands on" experience are unsurpassed. In my mind they are the right up there with the best in the World.

About The Author

Guy Edwards began his studies in Kung Fu in 1981 at the impressionable age of eight years old. Initially starting with Lau Gar (another Southern style originating from the Shaolin Temple and passed on through the "Lau Family") for a couple of years. Though his first exposure to Wing Chun came in 1983 under the tutelage of Master Austin Goh. Unfortunately the school closed down and he was forced to look elsewhere, which then brought him to Chang Kuen (Northern Long fist),Tong Long (Praying Mantis), and other Sil Lum (Shaolin) Boxing systems for the next few years.

After training with many Wing Chun instructors he settled with Hong Kong Grand Master (Victor) Kan Wah Chit (an original top student of the Late Grand Master Yip Man and senior Kung Fu brother to Bruce Lee) in London for several years.

He travelled hundreds of miles every week, for years, to train with an authentic source. And became the youngest student at twenty three to be authorised to teach for Sifu Kan.

He has also trained extensively in other Non-Chinese Martial Arts such as Filipino Arnis/Escrima, Indonesian Pencak Silat, Jun Fan/Jeet Kune Do, Intergrated Grappling Arts and Kickboxing.

Taking in countless courses, seminars, group and private tuition, with some of the Worlds best teachers. Guy is a registered Instructor with the British Chinese Martial Arts Council.

A group shot of Guy with some of his students in 1996 (V.K.V.T. Branch)

CONTENTS

CONTENTS

Introduction

Wing Chun Kung Fu is an explosive southern Chinese Boxing system that derives from the Shaolin Temple. It incorporates simultaneous attack and defence, evasive footwork, rapid hand combinations and powerful low line kicks. Based on logic and the bio-mechanics it is subtle yet highly sophisticated. Often confused for being just a "close range style" it also contains long range techniques.

Over the years there have been many books written on the subject of Wing Chun Kung Fu. With the exception of a few, the majority have been very informative, although most of them leave the reader with a lot of unanswered questions. Wing Chun has become so popular (and even controversial!) that many come to regard it as a Martial Art in itself like Karate, Tae Kwon Do, or Judo, rather than a style of Chinese Kung Fu.

This book is the first in a planned series and details important theories and key fundamentals that make up the building blocks of Wing Chun. I have included some other information on conditioning, making training equipment, eye focus drills, and correct kicking set ups which are not to be found in other books on the subject (I didn't want to "regurgitate" the data from previous publications on Wing Chun). I have also "peppered" this book with some of my favourite proverbs where I think applicable (these are not my own proverbs but ancient ones that I have borrowed). This book serves the reader with an insight into the Wing Chun classical 1ˢᵗ form of "Siu Nim Tau" and some of its applications.

I would like to point out that this book is only a guide and should not be taken for a substitute. You should seek out a genuine "Sifu" (or teacher) as trying to learn from books and videos will not give you the same scope as consistent training with a qualified instructor.

Remember: Practice Slow - Learn Fast!

Guy Edwards

1

A Brief History of Wing Chun

Wing Chun Kuen or Yong Chun Quan (Mandarin) translates as "Praise Spring" and Kuen (Quan) means "Style or Boxing". Where as the words Kung Fu or Gung Fu (Gong Fu in Mandarin) is a little more difficult to decipher, but it vaguely translates "Skill Effort" or more accurately "To attain skill through hard work".

Until recently the story as widely reported in other books and articles on Wing Chun, has been that the origins of the system stem from the 17th Century Buddhist Nun Ng Mui. There is no disputing the fact that there was a woman by the name of Ng Mui who lived in the 1600s and that her Martial Arts skills were legendary. In fact there is another system that can be traced to her and actually named after to her "Ng Mui Pai." But the story of her teaching a young orphan girl nicknamed "Yim Wing Chun" (roughly translates as "a new hope for the future") and then passing the system onto to her husband and so on to present day, is thought to be flawed.

The founder of Wing Chun Kung Fu may never be known, but a Master nicknamed "Tang Sau Ng" (because of his ability to control any attack through the usage of the Tang Sau "Palm up or Spread out arm") was understood to be pinnacle in the development of Wing Chun.

A discovery was found a few years back in some Chinese history chronicles detailing an account of a traveling opera troupe (by way of a big red "Junk" or barge). Hence they were called the "Hung Suen Hay Ban" (Red Junk Opera Company) and were instrumental in spreading the art that was being taught to them by "Tang Sau Ng." He was said to have masqueraded in costume and make up as a woman for the opera group. Was this where the rumour started?

This would then come down the line where it was to taught to Yip Man in the early part of the 20th century. He in turn would bring it from its birthplace of Faatsan to Hong Kong.

Stories were concocted to disguise the true origins of Wing Chun. This would be because all Martial Arts were banned by the Ching (Qing) dynasty due to the repressive regime. Many secret societies sprung up with the aim of over throwing them and reinstating the much less turbulent Han dynasty.

Although the records show Wing Chun flourished in Faatsan, Canton (renamed Foshan, Guangdong) Southern China, interestingly documentary evidence also mentions that "Tang Sau Ng" traveled to Faatsan from the North. (see Northern and Southern Influences)

Throughout history there have been well documented accounts of women creating and excelling in Martial Arts. This is true and not some mere fabled legend. Aside from the nun "Ng Mui" there were lots of female Masters as tough as any men. The creator of "Chuka" (Pheonix Eye) Kung Fu was a female. Outside of Chinese Martial Arts there are other styles said to be originated from women, for example Indonesian "Pencak Silat." Grand Master Floro Villabrille of Filipino "Arnis de Mano" was taught deadly techniques by a blind Princess (of all people) in the early part of the 1900s.

To this day female Grand Masters with direct lineages (usually through their families) still exist like the two sisters from Hong Kong; Grand Masters Lily & Gini Lau of the "Ying Jow Pai" (Eagle Claw) Kung Fu. Or the Indonesian Guru Ma Prem of Pencak Silat Wali Songo. This proves in itself that the idea of "weakness overcoming strength" is real! In fact from what I have seen tells me that women are actually faster learners than men when it comes to Wing Chun. They seem able to absorb the principles and energy points more easily.

PART 1
THEORY & PRINCIPLES

Laying the Foundation

The essence of attaining Kung Fu skill lies within the concept of building a strong foundation (similar to the structure of a house needing to stand up through years of varied weather conditions) which means plenty of time consuming and often boring but thoroughly necessary hard practice.

This is why Kung Fu should be taught in a very slow manner allowing each student to learn at his/ her own pace. It is often said learning Kung Fu is a life long journey of perfecting oneself and there is always another goal or level to be achieved. All Martial Arts have one thing in common and that is severe hardship to result in ultimate reality. In the early stages of training it is purely physical, but through perseverance, strong mental strength will be gained, from there it is possible to transcend to the higher levels spirituality (something every serious practitioner strives for).

The process of learning Wing Chun Kung Fu is akin to the learning cultivation of an elementary school, where first you are taught the alphabet representing the basics such as the: Stance, Punching, Kicking, etc; Then forming words could be compared to the training of more intermediate techniques like the practice of: Forms, Two Man Drills, Wooden Dummy etc; And then finally the construction and arrangement of sentences could be compared to the advanced training where you bring together everything. For example: Sparring, Fighting Applications, Weapons Training etc;

The beauty of Wing Chun is that if you have paid your dues with sweat and hard work in regards to "Laying the Foundation" then you will have very potent skills throughout your life even when very old.

"A journey of a thousand miles must begin with a single step"

Building Energies

All Chinese Martial Arts have their own methods for developing specialised powers or forces (known as Ging).

The Siu Nim Tau 1st form of Wing Chun as described later in this book is a "Gung Lik" or energy building metamorphical exercise, so to with the Dan Chi Sau Single Sticking Arm and the Poon Sau Double Rolling Arm drills. They all incorporate subtle pulling, clinging, and pressing energy forces.

Inch Force power is attained through repeated execution of Wall Bag training with wrist, elbow and hip conditioning. By tolerating contact and various levels of impact using a combination of self massage, bruising medicine, and specialised breathing techniques can help one to develop superior absorbing power resulting in rapid recovery.

In Wing Chun Kung Fu we do not use "Dead Energy" which could be described as using rigid brute force or unneeded muscle work. Instead we tend to rely on "Elastic Force" (Yau) which is a springy flexible power similar to a bamboo stick. The concept being that rigid artificial strength can snap where as the other is far more yielding and does not require too much physical exertion.

"A thousand hours practice for one minute's use!"

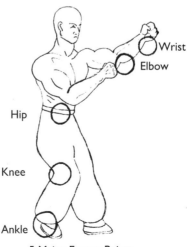

Wrist
Elbow
Hip
Knee
Ankle

5 Major Energy Points

Centreline Theory

One of the most important principles of the Wing Chun Kung Fu system is the Centreline Theory. The concept of this is not entirely unique as it can be found in many other styles including old English Boxing.

Imagine a long straight line going down the body where all of the major areas of attack can be found. Striking an opponent on the Centreline will upset their general equilibrium or balance due to the attack being fully absorbed, while any strike sustained outside of the Centreline would dilute or weaken an attack rather than maximise it.

For instance if someone gives you a hard shove on right side of your shoulder, you will find it is easy enough to roll with the movement in a deflective manner, the same with a punch to cheek which would no doubt hurt a lot more but like with the shoulder could be deflected by turning your head with the force. Now if someone gave you a shove to the chest however, you would immediately be sent reeling backwards as your body absorbs the force because of the central location, rather the than the left /right hand sides which are deflective.

So in Wing Chun we employ attacks to the opponent with a combination of both straight and angled strikes through the Centreline. By doing this it is less effort for creating force, which is why it is deemed as being so popular amongst smaller people who use skill instead of pure physical strength.

Economy of Motion

Every action and every movement in using Wing Chun Kung Fu should be made on sound logic, with the least amount of wastage in regards to technique efficiency and energy conservation. Co-ordinating the arms and legs to respond to an attack using this concept requires much practice to refine, not to mention common sense.

An example of this could be when someone delivers a strike high, you block and simultaneously hit them low and visa versa. So the general principle of the Economy Of Motion stresses absolute simplicity in conjunction with maximum performance, which is why Wing Chun is still perceived as highly functional and very effective.

Fighting multiple attackers is yet another reason for the importance of practical application as grappling with an opponent on the floor would only leave you exposed to attack from the others. An exercise you can use to aid contact reflex and basic response is "Mirroring or Mimicking" your opponents movement in training.

Arc Structure

Probably the strongest buildings ever made would have to be the Pyramids of ancient times, they have stood for thousands of years. The idea of standing in a posture that closely resembles an arc shape may seem slightly odd, but much like a building it has a solid structure that can not be bettered.

Pivoting the knees and feet inwards creates the shape of an Arc Structure and gives you the stability you need to stay on your feet during an assault. These days you are more likely to be attacked by multiple opponents, so taking a fight to the floor which is popular amongst grapplers might not be the best option. Also by keeping the Arc Structure you will maximise your hitting potential, see for yourself next time you watch a boxing match on the television. Notice how a professional boxer will employ a combination of bent knees and use pivoting feet to increase his stability and punching power. Look at "Goat Clamping Stance" for more information.

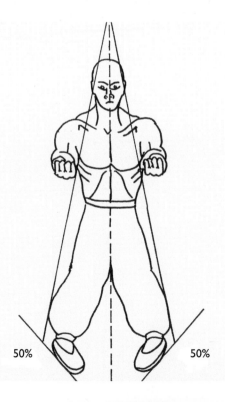

Six Gates of Attack

This relates to the idea of the opponent being divided into six main regions which are the upper, middle, and lower sections on the left and right hand sides. Thus by sectoring the regions into what is known as "Gates" it becomes much easier to break down any motion made when the opponent decides to attack.

The principle of using simultaneous attack & defence plays a key role for the practitioner of Wing Chun and this is one of the main reasons for the usage of the "Six Gates Of Attack & Defence". An example of this could be someone with an arm stretched out punching the head or upper gate would need to make sure the rest of their body would be amply protected, otherwise their opponent could easily take advantage of this by counter attacking with a low thrust to the shin or lower gate. Another example could be someone striking to the lower gate could be countered with a strike to the upper gate and so on. To think like this you need to try to visualise strongly that the attacker in front of you is not one unit but comprises six separate sections.

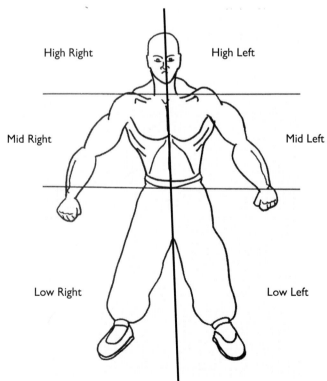

High Right   High Left

Mid Right   Mid Left

Low Right   Low Left

Simultaneous Attack and Defence

The main idea of this reverts back to the principle of the Economy of Motion in that all counter attacks should be both simple but effective. Using the Simultaneous Attack & Defence reduces the time scale in a fight rather than employing a block followed by a strike which is often favoured by other Martial Arts.

Wing Chun utilises combined movements by way of striking with either one hand or hand & foot while deflecting the on coming assault with the other arm.
The concept Yin (negative) &Yang (positive) play a vital role when using Simultaneous Attack & Defence. When attacked the practitioner slants (not leans!) their body away from the on coming power (Yin Force) reducing the momentum of their opponents strike. With this natural movement occurring, it becomes far more effective to send out simultaneous strike (Yang Force) with the other arm because of the slanting motion. The combined effect of the two forces create a feeling of drawing or sucking an opponent into your attack. (see Fighting Applications)

Golden Targets

(On Centreline)	(Off Centreline)
Forehead (extreme)	Temple (extreme)
Bridge of Nose	Eyes (extreme)
Under Nose (extreme)	Cheekbone
Upper Lip	Jaw Line
Chin	Neck (extreme)
Throat (extreme)	Floating Ribs
Sternum	Inside/Outside Elbow Joint
Solar Plexus (extreme)	Kidneys (extreme)
Lower Abdomen	Inside/Outside Thigh
Pubic Bone (extreme)	Inside/Outside Knee Joint
Groin (Extreme)	Inside/Outside Ankle Joint
Between Groin & Anus (extreme)	Feet & Toes

PART 2
WARM-UP DRILLS

Warm-up Exercises

The following set exercises are ideal for stretching the limbs and getting the blood circulation flowing. These exercises will improve your general speed and co-ordination needed for punching, kicking, and footwork. You should always take at least 10-15 minutes on warming up before embarking on any vigorous training, this is because you will find that standing in the "Goat Clamping Stance" for long periods of time puts an enormous amount of strain on legs and joints. I don't wish to put you off but in the beginning (if you are doing it correctly) your legs will feel like jelly!...and the same might be said for punching or kicking they all take their toll on the muscle tissue and joints.

What we are trying to attain is mainly upper torso flexibility but at the same time hips and legs must also be stretched. In fact nothing should be neglected with all areas being stretched including knees, ankles, fingers, and toes. It would be all to easy to fill this whole book with just stretching exercises alone but the ones illustrated here are the basic essentials for your improvement. Similar to a Chinese version of Yoga they should be performed slowly in a relaxed manner with normal breathing. In each exercise it is important that you actually feel the stretch occurring on the area you are working on and not just going though the motions. Be careful not to over exert yourself as this will naturally lead to some kind of muscle strain. The main reason for the development of "Soft" tendons, aside from being beneficial to ones health is to aid a fast recovery and prevent injuries. You might experience the noise of cracking bones while doing these exercises, this is perfectly normal and should be expected. Using "Tiger Balm" (red) or any other Bruise/Strain liniment before and after training helps to heat the muscles up and so too does taking a hot bath using Bath Salts. Try to supplement your diet with fish that are rich in Omega 3 oils (the fatty essentials) a couple of times a week as these have been proven to be good for supple limbs.

While it is true that Wing Chun revolves on skill and knowledge rather than physical prowess these exercises are the rudimentary basics essential for an all round better performance. All the exercises are performed standing up as it is good but not totally necessary to use the more vigorous leg stretching that would be needed for high kicking (as there are no high kicks in Wing Chun Kung Fu!)

Do the following exercises S-L-O-W-L-Y and repeat each movement on both sides
several times until you can do the stretch with all the postures.

Neck Exercises

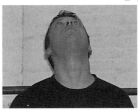

1. Tilt your head backward as far as possible.

2. Tilt your head forwards until your chin touches the top of your chest.

3. Turn your head fully to the right.

4. Then again to the left

5. Tilt your head to the right, making sure you keep your shoulders down.

6. Tilt your head to the left, again keeping your shoulders down.

7. Move your head in a circular motion with your chin touching your chest.

8. Repeat the movement again, but in the opposite direction.

Shoulder Exercises

1. Tilt your right shoulder in an upward motion.

2. Repeat the motion by pushing the left shoulder up and the right one down.

3. Make full circles with both shoulders using a forward action (sideview)

4. This time peel the backward to make full circle (sideview).

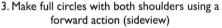

5. With the arms held straight, swing them forwards in a circular motion.

6. Repeat the process in a backward direction, again in full circles.

7. Co-ordinate one arm to go forwards, whilst the other goes backwards in full circles, and keep alternating.

Arm Exercises

1. Cup your right elbow with your left hand and pull back

2. Pull your right elbow across your left shoulder using your left hand

3. Put right arm under your left armpit and pull right elbow inwards

4. With your left hand pull your right elbow behind your back.

5. With an open hand and your palm facing up, pull your right elbow to the centre.

6. Bend right wrist back and rest on chest, using your left hand to pull your right elbow to the centre.

7. Put your right arm on top of your left and bend both arms in a folding manner until your hands are clasped

9. Wrap your right arm over your left shoulder and your left arm under your right armpit then use your fingers to move further up your back

10. Put your right arm behind the same shoulder and the left arm under the left side then clasp your hands behind your back.

Wrist and Finger Exercises

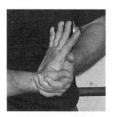

1a. With the left hand on the back of the right hand turn the wrist inward so the palm faces forward.

1b. Using a leverage action with the left hand push the fingers down and palm forward.

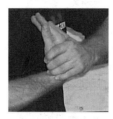

1c. Push the right wrist back towards you using the left hand to apply the pressure.

1d. Clasping the fingers of the right hand with the left raise the elbow and push the palm outwards.

2. Press each of the fingers back against each other as far as possible.

3a. With the hands pointing downward and elbows bent. Interlock the fingers so the palms are together.

3b. Rotate the wrists while maintaining the interlocked position so the hands point upwards.

3c. Finally with another turning of the wrists raise the interlocked hands above the head keeping elbows bent.

Hip Exercises

1. With your hands resting on your back and your knees slightly bent, lean and tilt your head back until you can see behind you.

2. Keeping your legs straight, lean forward and tuck your head in. Relax arm and neck muscles.

3. Place your palms together above your head and lean to the side.

4. Twist the torso while keeping your feet flat on the floor. Look between your hands until you can see behind you.

5a. With your hands on your hips rotate the waist in a circular motion with legs slightly apart.

5b. Repeat the process by rotating the waist in the opposite direction.

Hip Exercises

6a. Bend the right leg with your kneecap facing out and foot flat on the floor. Left leg held straight facing forward with heel bent back and hands behind your back. Inhale slowly through your nose.

6b. Lean forward keeping your hands behind your back and tuck your head in towards your front knee. Exhale slowly through your mouth.

6c. Lean to the side tucking the head in to touch the right kneecap. Exhale slowly through the mouth.

Leg Exercises

1a. Stand on one leg and pull your right knee across your chest with right arm. Keep your spine straight.

1b. Using your left arm pull the right knee across to the left while keeping shoulders and arms straight.

Leg Exercises

1c. Changing arms again pull your knee to the right side with your right arm.

1d. Point the right knee downward with the sole of the foot facing up, using the left arm to pull the foot up.

1e. Keeping the right knee pointing downward move across and push the foot forward with the right arm.

1f. Take the right foot behind with the left arm and pull upwards while pointing the knee downwards.

2a. Rest the right hand on the right thigh and the left hand on the left knee then lean forward keeping the rear leg stretched outward with torso upright.

2b. Crouch down with a backward movement keeping the right foot flat on the floor with your knee against your chest and keep the left leg straight out resting on the heel of the foot. Use your arms to balance yourself and tuck your head in.

Knees and Feet Exercises

1a. With the hands pushing on the kneecaps, bend the legs keeping your knees and feet together. Use a circular clockwise motion to work the stretch.

1b. Push the kneecaps back until the legs straighten. Then repeat the circular motion anti-clockwise. then push kneecaps back until the legs straighten.

2a. Lift the heel up and push the ankle forward while pressing the toes downward on the floor.

2b. With the heel on the floor turn the toes backward as far as possible.

2c. Pressing the outside edge of the foot against the floor turn the ankle so the underside of the foot raises.

2d. This time repeat vice versa by pressing the inside edge of the foot against the floor so the the underside raises.

Eye Focusing Drills

To focus on your opponents movements as they happen, you need to improve your eyesight. Developing your eye focusing skills to a high level can help you to achieve an almost "Sixth Sense" when it comes to hand to eye contact. Here are some drills to strengthen your retina and enhance your "Eye Focusing Energy" (Ngon Ging).

1) Close your eyelids shut, then without turning your head, look up, down, left, right, full circles clockwise and anti-clockwise, high corner left, right, low corner left, right. Do approximately ten of each then change. Also make sure you do a combination of both fast and slow movements. Note; Don't do this exercise for more than couple of minutes as it could induce a headache or strain the eyes.

2) Stand about ten feet away from your partner. With their arm held out straight in front of them, then ask them to make plenty of slow, fast and erratic movements with their hand. Your job is to follow their fingertips with the pupils of your eyes. All with moving the head.

3) Again stand about a ten foot distance away from your partner. Have him/her draw small letters in the air with their index finger. If they are too easy for you to decipher, then ask them to make the letters smaller including numbers.

4) This time have your partner stand about five away from your right hand side facing your ear. Then without turning your head, using your pheriphical vision only, try to decipher which punch they are throwing. Ask them to use variations of 2 & 3 (or more), with combinations of jabs, crosses, hooks and uppercuts.

Note: Do not use these exercises if you or your training partner has epilepsy.

Diet for Performance

If you eat right your body will function with clear regularity. Your sleep patterns will improve, which will lead you to having more concentration. Even your bowel movement will regulate. You will feel energised and you will get a strong sense of wellbeing. Also the improvement in your training will be dramatic. The very way we function our lives is governed by what we eat. It is all about your palate!

Here are some tips on how to improve your training performance through diet;

1) Eat clean foods. In other words plenty of fresh fruit, vegetables, berries, grains, pulses, nuts, herbs and spices (natural foods). Avoid processed and saturated foods like; cakes, biscuits, pies, chocolate etc;

2) Do not however deprive yourself of the occasional "naughty" hamburger, doughnut or whatever. If you limit it like this you enjoy it much more. "Nothing to excess"

3) Try to get a balance of protein, carbohydrates, fibre and vitamins. If you are "vegetarian" then make sure you have a good substitute in place of meat.

4) Eat lean meats. Cut any fat or skin off before cooking. Make sure you eat fresh fish a couple of times a week to keep your joints supple.

5) Drink purified water either from bought or by yourself with a "Water Purifier." Fruit juices, vegetable juices and herbal teas will all help to cleanse your body.

6) Rather than guzzling large amounts of liquid everyday try to eat more "Water based" fruit and vegetables such as; Melons, apples, pears, kiwi, oranges or cucumbers, tomatoes, marrows etc; Drinking too much water (or any other liquids) causes the internal organs to flood and will only you need the toilet more.

7) Always, always have "Breakfast." It is essential for your blood and oxygen supply to the brain. Skipping your first meal after sleeping (or fasting) can lead to poor lack of concentration. Make sure you mix protein and carbohydrates.

8) A couple of hours before vigorous training be sure eat some high energy foods. Also eat more carbohydrates and less protein, this will give you lots energy to "burn."

9) Thoroughly digest any food before embarking on any strenuous exercise. This very important to the blood sugar levels. Training on a full stomach can be detrimental.

10) Try to eat soon after any vigorous training session. More protein and less carbohydrate this time. Doing this will help aid your recovery, as protein repairs muscle tissue damage.

11) If you want to put on weight then you should mix protein and carbohydrates with all meals. This boosts the thyroid gland and provides the body with natural insulin.

12) If however you wish lose weight or strip fat then you should "up" the protein and cut "down" the carbohydrates. In conjunction to this exercise frequently. Never under any circumstances skip meals.

13) Try not to let yourself dehydrate when doing any vigorous training as you are bound to lose vast amounts liquid through sweat. Sip water (optional; with honey and lemon mixed) frequently. Do not guzzle as this can cause spasms and damage the lungs if out of breath.

14) Eat with regularity. Never skipping a meal. Don't let yourself get too hungry and at the same time do not eat until you are "bloated." Keep your meals frequent but moderate.

15) It's a good idea not eat after 9:00 in the evening as your "natural body clock" slows down. You need a chance to thoroughly digest your last meal before going to bed. Eating late will interfere with your sleep patterns as the food inside you will ferment where you are not burning calories.

Health and Fitness

Being physically in good shape does not mean you are healthy. Health is more about the state of your internal organs. Breathing exercises, Self massage of the "Accu Points," proper diet can all improve the health. The 1st form of Wing Chun "Siu Nim Tau" is a health building exercise.

It is also possible to have good health but poor physical fitness. Circuit training, swimming, weight training, sprinting etc; will all maximise your stamina levels.

Weight Training

Years ago the concept of using weight training to improve the Martial Arts ability was often frowned upon in various books and articles. The argument was that by doing so it only leads one to being slower in response to any attack. Not so! If you use weight training correctly in conjunction to Wing Chun, you can achieve phenomenal results in both speed and power.

The Shaolin Monks of ancient China used (and still do!) weight training to improve their power. The thing is weights should be used in Wing Chun to improve function rather than trying to make the body look more muscular. After all it is quite feasible for a smaller, slightly built person to have extraordinary strength. Only by gorging yourself with food do you get bigger.

PART 3
FUNDAMENTAL TRAINING

Correct Hand Positions

Here are a few little points on the correct formation of the fist and open hand as the incorrect position is a sign of sloppiness. Get used to opening and closing your hands as fast as possible.

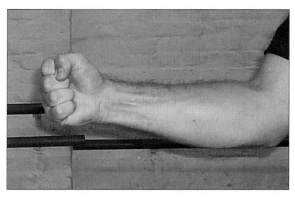

Fist: Make sure that your thumb covers the top two fingers when forming a fist. Never under any circumstances tuck the thumb underneath the fingers, as this could break your thumb or seriously damage your hand

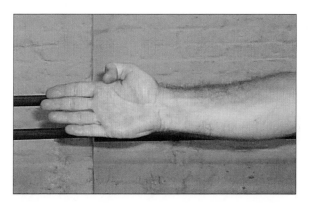

Open Hand: Make sure that your fingers are together, thumb tucked into the side and the palm flat when forming an open hand. Failure to do so could result in broken or dislocated fingers / thumbs in any vigorous contact situation.

Scenario Examples: Miss hitting, accidentally catching oneself on the attackers clothing, fighting a Jiu jitsu or Aikido practitioner (notorious for the finger / thumb breaks, locks and dislocations).

Goat Clamping Stance

Also known as the character two pressing stance it is the backbone to achieving stability and heavy striking power. Because of the unnatural structure of having both knees and feet turned inwards while in addition keeping the hips forward, spine straight and relaxed shoulder position can prove to be quite awkward in the early stages of learning. But like everything, it will become easier with time and practice to the point of staying in the posture for a prolonged period of time and actually developing a feeling of relaxation.

Back in the old days they would grip a live goat between their knees for as long as possible to gain awesome power in their stance (hence the long name "Goat clamping stance"). The stance represents a neutral state which is comfortable with abrupt changes able to move left, right, forward or backward with ease at any moment.

The principle to this would be similar to the game of Tennis, where the player does not commit to neither left nor right due to not knowing which direction the ball might come from. And so it would be the same if an attacker rushes in with a kick, punch, head butt or whatever to different areas of the body. The idea is to remain as uncommitted as possible and always ready for change.

Ready Position

1. Draw both fists up to nipple height, forearms straight and elbows pressing backwards, toes and feet slightly apart. Keep your shoulders relaxed through the entire sequence.

2. Keeping the knees together squat slightly and push the hips forward throughout the entire sequence.

3. Open the feet and knees simultaneously without lifting the heels or toes so they point outwards

4. Turn the knees inward and the heels outward simultaneously to complete the Goat Clamping Stance position

Finish

5. Adjust the right foot so it points forward

6. Draw the left leg inward along the floor until the feet and knees touch

Finish

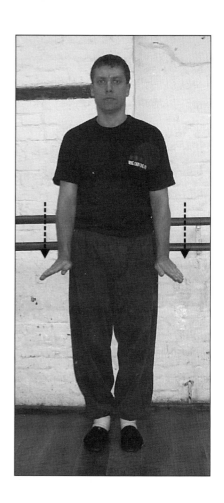

7. Turn the hands so the palms face downwards with the fingers pointing outwards. Keeping the elbows tucked back

8. Push your hands down the side of your legs, palms turned back as far as possible. Exhale slowly through the mouth with this motion.

On Guard

Holding the arms out in the On Guard position provides you with a fence or boundary lines which protects your main areas of weakness such as the head, ribs, stomach and groin. This should be kept at the correct distance as any over stretching of the arm might well lead you into being pulled into a barrage of strikes. Also by adjusting the arm too far back could well leave you vulnerable for a tackle to the ground or smothering movement. Keeping the arms placed too high could lead to either the stomach or groin being prone to attack and visa versa, if the arms are too low this could well leave your head, throat and chest area being exposed to attack.

Similar to the Goat Clamping Stance, the On Guard must be neutral in order for you to react immediately using the concept of the Six Gates of Attack and Defence. Think of your arms as a kind of ruler for measuring the distance between the fingertips of your extended hand and your opponents chin. One of key points with the On Guard is to maintain a permanent fixed elbow position with the extended arm, the reason being it makes sectoring your opponents strikes easier and more effective. The ideal gap between the chest and elbow can be measured by using the finger and thumb.

la. The forty five degree fixed elbow position.   Ib. The forty five degree fixed knee position.

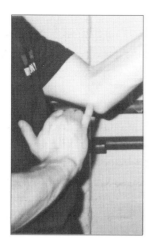

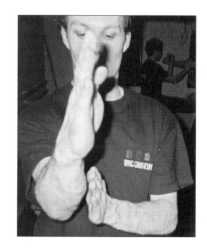

Distance between the elbow and the chest.

Distance of the gap between the front and rear hands.

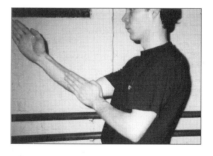

1. Line up the arms in an On Guard position.

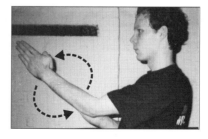

2. Switch rear hand over the top while retracting the front arm with smooth circular motion.

Straight Punch

The straight punch is performed sharp and fast, even afterwards when the punch or in fact any other strike is finished it should be retracted immediately. Failure to do so could lead to an opponent snatching the arm and therefore pulling the practitioner into an attack.

To develop dynamic punching power you must have a mixture of both air striking and contact striking on various textures to gain a feeling of impact. This will help you to build the certain group of muscles that are used for hitting with power and precision. To start with it is important to get the actual form of the punch correct making sure the angle is straight while speed and power will come later. Conditioning the knuckles on the Wall bag is also vital as this helps the practitioner develop "Inch force" (see Wall bag training).

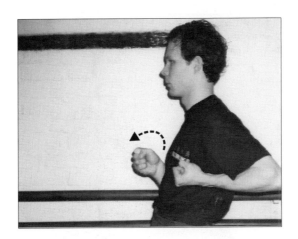

1. Hold your left fist cocked forward in front of your chest ready to launch the straight punch

Note: Exercise continued over the page

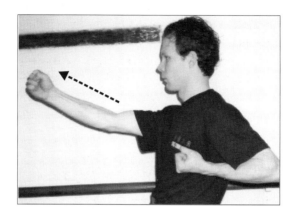

2. Thrust the punch out in a straight line, using your elbows and wrists simultaneously

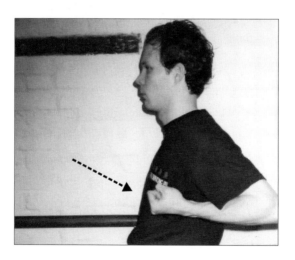

3. Immediately retract the punch by using a backward elbow strike

Note: The photo sequence above demonstrates the Noy Chung Choi inside straight punch coming from the centre of the chest. For the Ngoy Chung Choi outside straight punch merely move the ready position a few inches to the left side against the rib cage. (b) Thrust out the punch (c) draw back sharply as before.

Palm

The Palm can be very effective when executed in the right manner. To do this you must peel the palm back as far as possible upon launching from a relaxed position. The area of contact will be with the heel of the palm and this would be aimed at your opponents nose, chin, chest or in very extreme cases the forehead. Much like the punch or in fact any strike it is essential that the hands are conditioned by hitting the wall bag many times with the palms. Whenever using palm hits always ensure that your fingers are together and your thumbs tucked far back out of the way.

1. Place your hand in front of your chest with your palm facing downwards in the ready position

Note: Exercise continued over the page

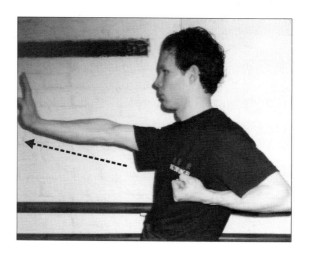

2. Thrust your hand out with your fingers pointing upwards. Turn your palm back as far as possible upon completion.

Side Palm

The Side Palm differs from the regular Palm in many ways such as the focus on maintaining the fixed elbow position from launch to execution. The entire area of the palm can be used and upon application the fingers can be curled slightly to create a sort of cup position.

Like the Palm the Side Palm keeps the thumb back to prevent breakage or dislocation and fingers tightly together for the same reason. Also the whole area of the hand must be angled to the side (neither pointing up nor down). Targets for Side Palm are usually chin, jaw line, floating ribs, or in extreme cases the kidney region.

1. Place your hand in front of your chest with your palm facing downwards in the ready position

Note: Exercise continued over the page

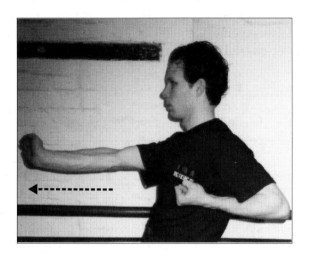

2. Thrust your hand out with your fingers pointing upwards. Turn your palm back as far as possible upon completion.

Centre Punching

This is similar to the idea of a sub-machine gun in that the name of the game is to fire out many punches with explosive speed, power and pinpoint accuracy. This is often but not always combined with forward attacking footwork thus making the Centre Punching powerful and very awkward to defend against.

There is no need to use any brute force as the whole concept of hitting the same target on exactly the same contact point over and over again proves highly effective. Apparently the late Bruce Lee had this technique down to a fine "T" through constant repetition and conditioning.

The main goal of Centre Punching is to knock the opponents balance or stability through barrages of well aimed hits usually to the chin area. Each and every punch must be kept as straight as possible, but then a very small semi-circle follows immediately after when loading the fist back to a cocked position next to the elbow ready for the launch of the next straight punch. A common mistake by some Wing Chun practitioners is punching one over the top in circular fashion which unfortunately is both easy to counter and lacks the same power of a straight punch.

1. Thrust a straight punch outwards, while cocking the left fist near the right elbow joint ready to punch again

2. Repeat the process by snapping the left wrist and elbow simultaneously until locked straight. Immediately retract the right fist near to the left elbow ready to punch again

Front View: Punch along the centre line. Your rear arm is poised ready to punch again, elbow pointing downwards and arm against your rib cage. Shoulders relaxed throughout

PART 4
FOOTWORK

Effective Kicking

The Wing Chun style employs only a small number of kicks in comparison to other systems where vast amounts of kicking techniques can be found. In fact there are only eight kicks (although some of them are leg obstructions and foot trips rather than kicks) which are all delivered no higher than waist height and are highly functional.

While hand techniques make up the core of the system, kicking and footwork are also very important for gaining full control of an assailant. Some of the kicks are not used to pulverise your opponent, but more to distract them while you blast them with a hand combination (this is known as "invisible kicking"). Apart from the groin being the most favourable area to kick, the inside and outside knee joint / ankle joint / hip / thigh and shin are also viable targets. Here are several reasons why high kicks could be impractical in violent situation.

a) You need plenty of space to execute a high kick successfully
b) Someone could easily evade your kick if you are not quick enough
c) Upon landing you are vulnerable to counter attacks and leg sweeps
d) You might not be agile enough at the time needed for the kick
e) Environment could hamper a high kick i.e.; you might be on a slope, in a lift, walking up steps, on snow, gravel etc;
f) Your foot or leg could be grabbed leaving you at risk to falling over or being kicked in the groin.

Footwork and kicks are more intermediate and make up a lot of the training to be found in Chum Kiu Searching the Bridge phase of Wing Chun Kung Fu (to be detailed in the following book). Here I have shown the correct set up, execution and finish for the front and side kick, these are the key to the power development and are the building foundation for other kicks.

Knee Raise

Side View

1a. Toes three inches apart and heels one inch apart, with your knees pointing slightly outwards.

1b. With one fast movement raise your knee to your chest area and turn your heel back as far as possible.

Side View

1a. Lean back slightly ready to lift your leg to the ready position.

1b. Maintain the upper body position and keep supporting leg bent.

Note:
Practice your balance thoroughly before moving onto the Front Kick. Build up the duration of time each time on each leg lift and always fight to keep your balance even if you wobble around. If you keep dropping your leg every time you lose your balance you will never learn.

Front Kick

1. From the Goat Clamping Stance, hold the arms out in an On Guard position.

2. Turn your right heel inwards, so that your toes point outwards.

3. Keeping the supporting leg bent, raise your left knee as far as possible.

4. Snap out your leg so your kneecap locks straight. Turn your heel back as far as possible to complete a Ding Gerk - Front Nailing Kick

5. Upon completion of the front kick put your foot down immediately with a stamp, landing with your foot angled inwards.

6. Adjust your foot back into the Goat Clamping Stance.

Turn and Kick

1. From the Right Forward Stance, hold the arms out in an On Guard position.

2. Turn your head as far as possible and use your eyes to focus on the direction of attack.

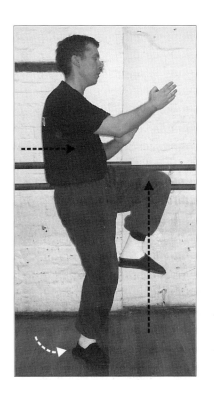 

3. With a smooth sweeping action turn your feet, hips and torso in unison while simultaneously lifting your left knee.

4. Execute a Front Kick by locking your left kneecap, with heels turned back as far as possible. Keep your supporting leg bent.

Side Kick

1. From the Goat Clamping Stance, hold the arms out in the On Guard position.

2. Turn your left heel inwards and lean the body over to the left hand side while straightening the right leg. Turn your head to the direction of attack

3. With one quick movement lift your knee in front of your chest horizontally ready to execute a Side Kick. Keep the supporting leg locked straight.

4. Thrust out the right leg while keeping the foot turned fully to the side until the kneecap locks straight to complete a Wang Gerk - Side Kick

5. After executing the Side Kick put the right foot immediately with a stamp, landing with the foot turned inwards

6. Adjust the left foot back to the Goat Clamping Stance.

Forward and Backward Shuffle

This is a basic footwork drill that can be used in conjunction with Centre Punching when moving forward and with Slapping Hand or On Guard position when moving backward.

The Forward and Backward Shuffle or Jull Ma - Running Horse should be executed in a straight line. Keep the shoulders parallel with the hips pushing forward, but avoid leaning forward with the back when moving.

After a few attempts you should be able to abandon looking down at your feet to check your position, keeping your head upright and eyes looking ahead. If moving backward look over your shoulder every so often to make sure there are no obstructions.

1. Have both knees bent with the rear leg at 60% and your lead leg at a 40% weight distribution

2. Edge your lead foot forward slightly then follow up by sliding the rear foot immediately leaving a small gap.

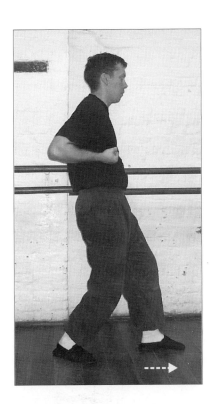

3. Repeat the process by nudging forward with a fast tight shuffle.

4. To move backward just change to visa versa. Edge the rear foot first followed by the lead foot and so on.

Turning Punch

The structure of the Turning Punch is similar to the cross punch in boxing where the attack is thrown in a straight line but delivered at an angle. To execute this effectively you must use a combination of punching, turning of the hips, and turning of the feet simultaneously to maximise momentum.

Before launching the punch it is necessary to turn the head and focus with the eyes on the direction of the target which is usually the jaw line, cheekbone or in extreme cases the side of forehead.

By exhaling from the mouth sharply upon making contact even more explosive power can be attained. The crossing of the arms between the set up provides a protection cover for the upper and mid section.

1. With feet and knees angled to the right simultaneously thrust out a right straight punch slightly to the side. Do not lean, use the hips and shoulders as one unit.

2. Turn your head to the left and use your eyes to focus on the direction of the next attack.

3. As you begin to turn your feet bring your left arm through, making a cross shape to provide protective cover.

4. Complete the turn by moving the whole foot area. Thrust out a left straight punch slightly to the side. Do not lean or slant, use the hips and shoulders in unison.

Twist Side Punch

This is an extension to the Turning Punch with difference of using a fuller turning motion in conjunction with the punch. The 180 degree turn means that you can strike an opponent who attacks you from behind with speed and efficiently. It is important that you focus on the target before committing to the punch, aside from turning the head you need to turn the eyes fully to maximise your vision behind you.

Both the Turning Punch and the Twist Side Punch can be thought of as heavy artillery similar to the large cannon. By utilising all of the power sources like the elbow, hips and legs knockout punching can be achieved.

1. Right foot turned fully to the side, left foot angled slightly. Shoulders and hips fully turned to the side with a straight punch

2. Without moving the upper and lower posture, turn your head as far as possible using your eyes to focus on the direction of attack.

3. As you begin to turn, retract your left punch and use your right forearm to make a cross shape to provide a protective cover.

4. Complete the turn fully while simultaneously using a straight punch. When retracting, the elbow becomes a powerful backward strike. Do not lean or slant, use the hips and shoulders in unison.

Part 5
Equipment

Using Equipment

Use Focus Mitts to train the simultaneous attack and defence drills. You can practice literally hundreds of different combinations to improve your hand and eye co-ordination and by doing so you will gain a sense of impact.

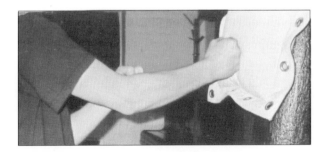

Condition ing the fists on a Wall Bag will help you to cultivate Chuen Ging - Inch Force Power. This will enhance your ability to make an explosive punch from a very short distance.

Wallbag Training

1. Stand less than arms length away in front of the Wall Bag in the Goat Clamping Stance.

2. With your right elbow pointing downwards and the arm pressing against the rib cage, cock the fist in front of the chest ready to punch.

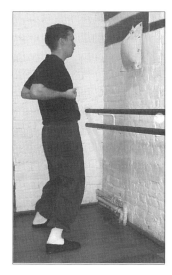

3. Thrust out a straight Inside Punch into the Wall Bag using the bottom three knuckles. Leave the fist to absorb the impact for a couple of seconds before punching again.

Hand Conditioning

To attain powerful striking it is most necessary to temper the hands by way of hitting wall bags, focus mitts, punch bags and anything else that will give a feeling of impact. It is just as important though to use caution with this type of training, as not to sustain permanent damage to your hands (which could result in arthritis). So in the early stage you can expect some kind of soreness or bruising but in time you will feel your tolerance levels adjust and hands will begin to toughen.

Like the "Arm Conditioning" it is recommended that anyone who conditions the hands on the wall bag should use a decent "Bruising Medicine". The ingredients or filling for a wall bag should be 70% fine gravel and 30% dried soya beans (which are sold by most health shops). When mixed together they provide a texture similar to the feeling of hitting bone and tissue. Many practitioners use sand in their wall bags but this is not as effective as the gravel and soya bean mixture described . The wall bag being canvas plays a major role in strengthening the skin to a leather like consistency, it is common to split skin on the knuckles in early stages.

Distance is also essential as standing at arms length will not give you any real power, by standing nearer the wall bag (almost but not quite half way) "Inch Force" can be developed. The wall bag differs from focus mitt or punch bag training as it employs a slow heavy pounding and is not for speed combinations or timing. Bag gloves should be worn when using either focus mitts or punch bags as this prevents damage your knuckles and wrists.

Wrist Roller

1. Hold the Wrist Roller Weight (see making training equipment) at shoulder height with the elbows locked straight, standing in the Goat Clamping Stance.

2. Without bending the elbows use the wrists fully several times to ravel up the weight to the top of the bar, before repeating the drill again.

1. Stand on one leg with the knee near the chest and foot turned back as far as possible. Supporting leg bent and the arms held out with the elbows locked straight.

2. Without moving from the spot use the wrists fully several times to ravel up the weight to the top of the bar, before repeating the drill again.

Punching with Weights

1. Hold a small dumbbell or hand weight (see making equipment) in the right hand next to the right side of the chest in a Goat Clamping Stance.

2. Turn the knees, feet and hips simultaneously while using the hand weight to deliver a Turning Punch

1. Standing in a Goat Clamping Stance cock the fist so it points forward while holding the hand weight.

2. Thrust out a straight Inside Punch using the wrist and elbow in unison, before retracting the arm to punch again.

Making Training Equipment

There are a few vital apparatus that are not available from Martial Arts retailers. Here are some tips on making some essential training equipment on a budget. All of these are very simple to make and the materials can be purchased easily.

Hand Weights

Use these to enhance your speed and power with punches. They are perfect for Centre Punching because they will not get in the way, like the top and bottom of a small dumbbell. Another plus is they are just the right weight as using heavier weights to punch with actually reduce the skill we are trying to develop here.

1. Take a stack of the same size large coins (low denomination will be cheaper)

2. Line up the stack and wrap strong carpet or duct tape around them tightly several times. Make another for your other hand to hold.

3. There should be a little extra visible at the top and bottom when held in the fist. They are now ready for punching practise. Repeat 50 punches in each hand.

Wrist Roller Weight

This will strengthen your gripping power needed for various Lop Dar (Grabbing Arm) and Chin Na (Seize and Control) drills. It will also build the sinew and tendon in the forearms increasing the weight of your strikes.

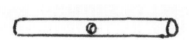

1. Drill a hole in the centre of a 2ft piece of thick dowling rod (a section of broom handle can be used instead).

2. Tie a single small weight from a barbell or small bag of gravel (remember not too heavy) with a 3ft piece of rope.

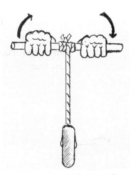

3. Feed the other end of the rope through the hole in the stick and then tie. Hold it out in front of you at shoulder height with elbows locked straight. Ravel / unravel the weight several times until the arms are exhausted.

Towel and Bowl

This ancient technique will build similar attributes as the Wrist Roller Weight. It will also strengthen the fingers for clawing and gouging techniques.

1. Find a large towel made from thick material (cotton is best).

2. Fill a bucket or washing bowl three quarters full of water.

3. Practice ringing the water out of the towel by using a twisting action. Try to drain every drop of water out of the towel. Repeat the process until the forearms burn.

Swinging Kick Bag

The Swinging Kick Bag differs greatly from the usual type of Thai Pad, Punch Bag or Kick Shield sold by Martial Arts retailers. Kicking a sack of gravel may seem crude, but by doing so you will develop masses of power for executing front and side kicks. The swinging motion will provide you with strong calf, thigh and buttock muscles while toughening the sole of the foot.

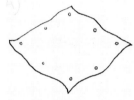

1. Take a 3ft square piece of canvas then make a small hole about two inches away from the edge in each of the four corners.

2. Place approximately 10kg of fine gravel (fish tank size) in the middle of the canvas. Bring each of the four corners up then use some thick string to weave in and out of the holes. Tie together to create a sack like shape.

3. Wrap some rope around the neck of the bag several times and tie. Find somewhere to secure the other end of the bag so that it swings. Practice your kicks slowly without any power at first and then over the next few months increase speed and power gradually. Repeat 50 times with each leg.

Swinging Bag

To cultivate explosive Side Palms, Chops and condition the forearms to new levels you should use a Swinging Bag instead of a conventional Wall Bag. Like the Swinging Kick Bag it employs a swaying motion rather then being stationary.

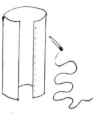

1. Using a piece of canvas about arms length, fold to create a cylinder shape and then sew it up securely (or cut the trouser leg of an old pair of jeans).

2. Tie the bottom of the bag several times with rope. Fill the bag up till bulging with fine gravel (fish tank size). Leave enough room to tie the top tightly with rope (remember: you don't want the bag bursting).

3. Attach the end of the rope securely to something so it provides you with a swinging motion.
Practice the Side Palm very lightly at first, just enough to make the bag swing back and forth. Only increase momentum after a few weeks (do not underestimate this bag). Repeat 50 times with each hand.

Rubbing Stake

By slapping the palms on a large wooden stake you can condition your hands to a devastating effect. But you must approach this drill softly and use very little power upon striking it for some time. Then after a few weeks of this, gradually increase the power of your slaps. Any hard slaps before the hands are ready could do permanent damage to the nerves in your hands, so go L-I-G-H-T-L-Y. This training develops the practitioners striking ability by making the arms feel very heavy upon contact.

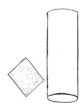

1. Cut a 3ft section of a wooden stake making sure it has a round circumference (you can use a tree log if available). Rub the stake down with sandpaper until smooth to prevent any splinters in the hand

2. Hammer four hooks equally spaced apart around the side near the top of the stake.

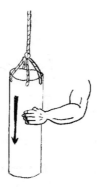

3. Feed rope through the hooks and tie together. Tie the end of the rope to something secure so that the stake swings. Forming a cup shape with the hand, pat the Rubbing Stake gently then without taking the hand away immediately slide off with smooth motion (Remember no power yet).   Repeat 50 times with each hand.

Iron Slap Bag

Like the Rubbing Stake the Iron slap bag will greatly improve your Paak Sau (Slapping Arm) blocks and strikes. Yet again caution needs to be used with this as pounding your hands before they are ready will have a counter effect on what we are doing. The ingredients can be changed from gravel to pebbles and then lead shot or ball bearings as you improve.

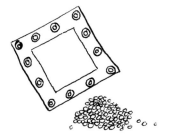

1.Purchase a Wall Bag and fill it with fine gravel (fish tank size) till bulging. (a duffle bag can be used).

2.Fold the corners in and wrap the bag tightly with either strong carpet or duct tape.

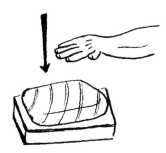

3. Place the parcel shaped bag on a block of wood to provide a platform. Practice slapping the bag from a distance of no more than 1ft (Go slow just patting it lightly and you will get good results in a short time).   Repeat 50 times with each hand

Part 6

Little Idea
1st Form

Siu Nim Tau
Little Idea

Comprised of six main sections the 1st form of Wing Chun Kung Fu is performed entirely in a stationary "Goat Clamping Stance" fixture. Throughout all the form concentration is placed on correct alignment of the arm positions and relaxed breathing.

Many kinds of variations exist of this pattern, with the majority looking very similar but with subtle differences. The reasons for the practicing of this form have a multiple purpose in that you are building unique group areas of sinew and muscle which allow you to develop both elasticity and massive strength without usage of crude weight training. This is apparent in the second part of the form where the practitioner takes a very long time to move back and forth in the palm up and cover arm position while using dynamic tension. This is what is known as "stillness within motion" or to put it another way there is constant movement but it is so very slow that it appears as if stationary.

Every single movement in the "Little Idea" has a meaning or application and should not be just considered as merely a combination of fancy moves that are performed in the air. Regard it as a strength building form of standing meditation and you will come to understand why it is recognised as the most important phase of training in Wing Chun.

This is the key to the to next important stage of the "Single & Double Sticking Arms". The 1st form should take at the very minimum fifteen minutes to perform (the bulk of which is the second section) but the longer you spend on it tthe better, as the essence is on patience. If you can, try to do the form near plenty of trees and bushes, so you get lots of clear oxygen.

Section 1

1. With the legs together raise both fists up to the ready position.

2. Keeping the legs together and the back straight, bend the knees.

3. Open the knees and feet so they point outwards.

4. Turn the knees and heels so they point inwards to perform a Yee Jee Kum Yueng Ma - Goat Clamping Stance.

5. Thrust hands down to make a cross shape with the left arm folded on top of the right arm (pressing together firmly).

6. Without separating the arms raise up to make a cross shape near the face right arm folded over the top of the left arm this time (press together firmly).

89

7. Draw both fists back sharply.

8. Thrust a left Noy Chung Choi - Inside Straight Punch, shoulder height.

9. Keeping the elbow locked straight open hand and turn palm face up.

10a. Bunch all fingers together to touch thumb. Bend the wrist upwards as far as possible.

10b. Keeping the wrist bent back turn hand slowly and smoothly so the fingers and thumb point downward to complete a left Huen Sau - Circling Hand

11. Form a fist.

12. Draw the left fist back sharply.

13. Thrust a right Noy Chung Choi out at shoulder height.

14. Keeping the elbow locked straight, open the hand and turn palm face up.

15a. Bunch all fingers together to touch thumb. Bend wrist upwards as far as possible.

15b. Keeping the wrist bent, turn the hand slowly and smoothly so the fingers and thumb point downward to complete a right Huen Sau

16. Form a fist.

17. Draw the right arm back sharply.

Now complete the entire sequence of section 2 on the right hand side.

Section 2

1. Open the left hand palm facing up.

2. Begin to move the hand out very slowly to make a Tang Sau - Palm up arm.

3a. Without moving the forearm, begin to turn the hand with fingers pointing inwards. Wrists back as far as possible.

3b. Complete a left Huen Sau - Circling Hand slowly and smoothly. Continue the hand to form a Wu Sau - Praying arm. (pause before moving again).

4. Begin to move the Wu Sau back in a straight line, an inch away from the chest, very slowly (pause before moving again).

5. Without moving the forearm bend the left wrist back as far as possible, all fingers bunched together touching the thumb to form a Fok Sau - Controlling arm (pause before moving).

6. Push the Fok Sau forwards keeping the elbow turned inwards, till one inch from the chest, very slowly (pause before moving again).

7a. Without moving the forearm, begin to turn the hand with fingers pointing inwards. Wrist back as far as possible.

7b. Complete a second left Huen Sau slowly and smoothly. Continue turning the hand to form a second Wu Sau (pause before moving again).

8. Begin to move the Wu Sau back in a straight line, an inch away from the chest, very slowly (pause again).

9. Without moving the forearm bend the left wrist back as far as possible, all fingers bunched together to form a second FokSau (pause)

10. Push the Fok Sau forwards keeping the elbow turned inwards, till one inch away from the chest, very slowly (again pause before moving).

11a. Without moving the forearm, begin to turn the hand with fingers pointing inwards. Wrist bent back as far as possible.

11b. Complete a third left Huen Sau slowly and smoothly. Continue turning the hand to form a third Wu Sau (pause before moving again)

12. Begin to move the Wu Sau back in a straight line, an inch away from the chest, very slowly (pause again).

13. Without moving the forearm bend the left wrist back as far as possible, all fingers bunched together to touch the thumb to form a third and final Fok Sau (pause again before moving)

14. Push the Fok Sau forwards keeping the elbow turned inwards, till one inch away from the chest, very slowly (pause before moving again).

15a. Without moving the forearm, begin to turn the hand with fingers pointing inwards. Wrist bent back as far as possible.

15b. Complete the fourth and final left Huen Sau slowly and smoothly. Continue turning the hand to form the fourth and final Wu Sau (pause before moving on again).

16. Begin to move the Wu Sau back in a straight line, an inch away from the chest, very slowly (pause before moving again).

17. Move the left palm abruptly to the left side, in line with the shoulder to form a Paak Sau - Slapping Arm.

18. Spring back to the Wu Sau position, ready to execute a left palm strike.

19. Thrust out a left Juerng - Palm

20. Keeping the elbow locked straight, open the hand and turn the palm face up.

21a. Bunch all fingers together to touch thumb. Bend the wrist upwards as far as possible.

21b. Keeping the wrist bent, turn the hand slowly and smoothly so the fingers and thumb point downward to complete a left Huen Sau

22. Form a fist.

23. Draw the left arm sharply.

Now complete the entire sequence of section 2 on the right hand side.

Section 3

1a. Open the hand and turn the left palm so it faces downwards.

1b. With the left hand, brush down the left side of the leg against the trousers, palm back as far as possible and fingers pointing forward to complete a Gum Sau - Pinning Arm.

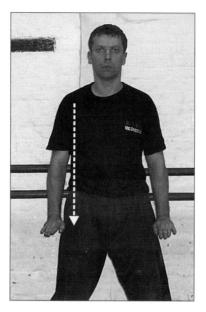

2. Immediately follow this with a right Gum Sau brushing down the side of trouser leg.

3. Raise both hands and put behind the back as high as possible without lifting the shoulders.

Rear View

3. Fingers pointing downwards and thumbs touching together.

5/.

4. Thrust both hands outwards behind your back to complete a Suerng Gum Sau - Double Pinning Arm

4. Palms back as far as possible. Keep the thumb close together and do not lean forward.

5a. Keeping the hands flat in front of the chest, bend the wrists so the fingers point downward ready to per form a Suerng Gum Sau.

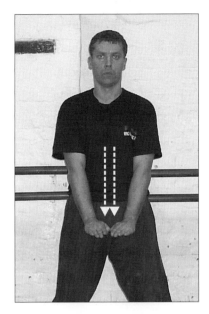

52

5b. Thrust both palms downward with the thumbs touching together in front of the groin to complete a Suerng Gun Sau.

53

6. Fold the left arm one inch over the top of right arm at nipple height to make a Suerng Lan Sau - Double Barring Arm.

115

7. Open the arms outward horizontally to make a Suerng Chan Sau - Double Chopping Hand

8. Fold the right arm one inch over the top of the left arm at nipple height to make a second Suerng Lan Sau.

9A. Without separating the arms fold into a cross shape ready to perform a Suerng Man Sau - Double Asking Hand.

9B. Open the arms and pull the elbows backwards in a jolting motion, one inch away from the chest palms facing inwards to complete a Suerng Man Sau - Double Asking Hand.

10. Keeping the elbows near each other turn the wrists so the palms are facing up to make a Suerng Tang Sau - Double Palm Up Arm.

56

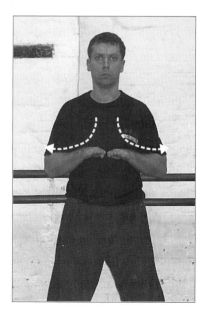

11. Pull back the hands and turn the wrists so the palms face downwards with a second jolting motion. Keeping the thumbs together to make a Suerng Jum Sau - Double Jerking Arm.

12. Thrust both hands outwards at shoulder height to make a Suerng Biu Jee - Double Darting Fingers.

13. Keeping the elbows locked straight push both arms downward in front of groin with the palms bent back as far as possible and the together thumbs touching to make Suerng Gum Sau.

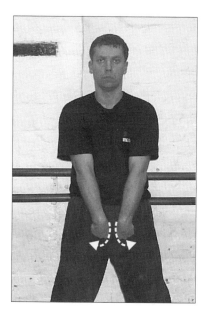

14a. With the fingers bunched together all touching the thumb bend the wrists inwards ready to perform a Suerng Fok Sau - Double Controlling Arm.

14b. Swiftly raise both arms at shoulder height with wrists bent inwards and fingers pointing downwards to complete a Suerng Fok Sau.

15. Close both hands to form fists.

16. Draw both arms back sharply.

17. Move the left palm abruptly to the left side, in line with the shoulder to form a Paak Sau.

18. Spring back to the Wu Sau position ready to execute a left side palm.

19. Thrust out a left Wang Juerng - Side Palm

20. Keeping the elbow locked straight, open the hand and turn the palm face up.

21. Keeping the elbow locked straight open hand and turn palm face up.

22a. Bunch all fingers together touching thumb. Bend the wrist upwards as far as possible.

124

22b. Keeping the wrist bent, turn the hand slowly and smoothly so the fingers and thumb point downward to complete a Huen Sau.

23. Form a fist.

24. Draw the left arm in sharply.

Now repeat the last few motions on the right hand side:
Paak Sau / Wu Sau / Wai Jueng / Huen Sau and Draw

Section 4

1.Keeping the elbow inwards with palm facingup thrust out a left Tang Sau

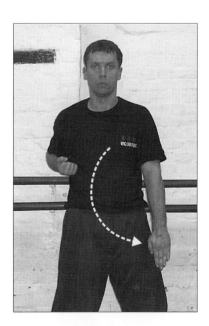

2.With an arc like movement sweep the left hand downward in front of the left leg to make a Garn Sau - Cultivating Arm.

3. Keeping the elbow inwards with the palm facing up raise the left arm to make another Tang Sau.

4. Without moving the elbow position, bunch all fingers together to touch thumb. Bend the wrist slowly and smoothly to make Huen Sau.

5. From the Huen Sau motion turn the palm back and fingers to the side ready to launch a left side palm.

6. Thrust a left Wang Juerng.

7. Keeping the elbow locked straight, open the hand and turn palm face up.

8a. Bunch all fingers together touching the thmb. Bend the wrist upwards as far as possible.

8b. Keeping the wrist bent, turn the hand slowly and smoothly so the fingers and thumb point downwards to complete a Huen Sau.

9. Form a fist.

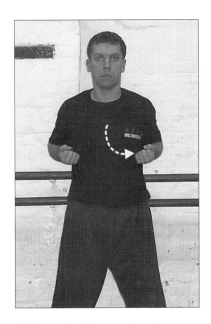

10. Draw the left arm in sharply.

Now repeat the entire sequence of section 4 on the right hand side

Section 5

1. Open the left hand palm face up.

2. With the left wrist lower than the elbow and shoulder relaxed, use a cork screw motion to form a Bong Sau - Wing Arm.

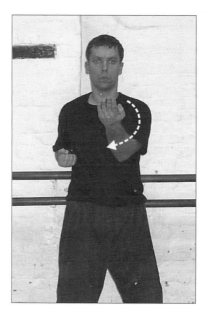

3. Immediately follow this by turning the arm so the left elbow is in and the palm is facing up to make a Tang Sau.

4. With wrist bent forward as far as possible thrust the palm out with fingers pointing downwards to execute a Dai Juerng - Low Palm at shoulder height.

5. Turn the left wrist back so the entire hand and arm lock straight.

6a. Bunch all fingers together touching the thumb. Bend the wrist upwards as far as possible.

6b. Keeping the wrist bent, turn the hand slowly and smoothly so the fingers and thumb point downwards to complete a Huen Sau

7. Form a fist.

8. Draw the left arm in sharply.

Now repeat the entire sequence of section 5 on the right hand side

Section 6

1. Left arm pointing downwards with palm facing in. Back of the right hand resting on the left elbow joint area.

2. Brush the back of right hand along the left forearm and turn the palm inwards, while immediately retracting the back of the left hand to the right elbow to form a Tut Sau - Freeing Arm.

3. Brush the back of the left hand along the right forearm and turn the palm inwards, while immediately retracting the back of the right hand to the left elbow area to form a second Tut Sau.

4. Brush the back of right hand along the left forearm and turn the palm inwards, while immediately retracting the back of the left hand to the right elbow to form a third and final Tut Sau.

5. Keeping the right arm stationary turn the left hand to form a fist in a cocked position ready to launch a punch.

6. Retract the right arm while thrusting out the left fist to execute a Lien Wan Choi - Centre Punch.

7. Repeat a second Lien Wan Choi with the right fist.

8. Repeat a third and final Lien Wan Choi with the left fist.

9. Draw both arms in sharply.

10. Turn the left foot slightly till pointing straight.

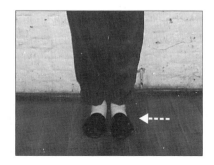

11. Draw the right leg inwards to touch the left leg using a sweeping action.

12. Turn hands so palms face downwards.

13. Push both palms downward and breathe out slowly.

Authors Note: Other Wing Chun schools may use more movements or do things different in their 1ˢᵗ form, but this does not mean they practicing some secret motions that I have forgot to include here. That's just their individual way of performing Siu Nim Tau. Example; sometimes a Tarn Sau-Bounce off hand is used to finish various sections (straight after the Paak Sau and just before whichever strike). Slow graceful lifting of the Suerng Fok Sau position in the third section. Extra Wu Sau or Jum Sau motions in the fourth section. Speeding up and slowing down throughout the form. More Centre Punching or a final Huen Sau at the end. Other common traits might be the dipping motion upon drawing the fist back or angling the fists upwards upon punching. They may also number their sections differently or use a different spelling to that of Siu Nim Tau.

Circling Hand Keys

Side View

1. Wrist and elbow locked straight, palm facing upward. Shoulder height.

2. Bend the wrist back as far as possible while bunching all the fingers together to touch the thumb (like the Fok Sau hand).

3. With one smooth action rotate the wrist so the fingers and thumb point downwards.

4. From this position form a fist.

5. Draw back the arm sharply.

Authors Note: Other Wing Chun school may use a fuller rotation of the hand, sometimes turning the fist upwards before drawing. Also they may use open fingers as opposed to the closed bunched (Fok Sau hand shape).

Third Section Keys

Side View

1. From the Fok Sau position apply the dynamic tension to the forearm.

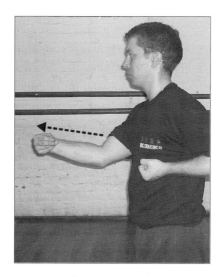

2. Begin to move the Fok Sau forward ultra slowly applying the tension throughout.

3. Take the tension off and rotate the wrist from the Fok Sau position to a Wu Sau with one smooth action

4. Pause then reapply the dynamic tension to the forearm.

5. Begin to move the Wu Sau inward ultra slowly applying dynamic tension throughout..

Authors Note: Move the arm like a typewriter; stopping, locking, starting etc; Try not to over strain the arms while doing this. Other Wing Chun schools may use higher hand positions and replace the Wu Sau for a Jum Sau throughout this section.

PART 7
TWO MAN DRILLS

Two Man Drills

Training with a partner is absolutely vital to the development of a practitioner in   order to get a sense of reality and for improving your attributes such as speed, timing, co-ordination etc; But training with the same person without change might steer the practitioner towards a comfort zone and could hinder progress.

Two Man Drills should be practiced with if possible a broad mixture opponents such as smaller, taller and same heights/ lighter, heavier and same weight categories / weaker, superior and same skill levels. There is a old proverb that relates to this "Tools sharpen on stone, Man sharpens on man".

Arm Conditioning

This is vital for generally toughening ones forearms on both inside and outside radius, the purpose being to enable you to absorb strong attacks such as punches and kicks with very little or even no sustained injuries. Sometimes referred to as "Three Star" (Sarm Sing/Gat Sau) it can be found in almost every system of Kung Fu with some slightly different variations of course.

When starting the arm conditioning drill you must pay constant attention to the area of impact which is located just above the top wrist but not the actual wrist itself and special attention should be given to breathing as normally as possible. It has to be said that it can be very painful in the earlier stages of training and bruises can and will be expected, therefore it is suggested that you find a decent bottle of "Bruising Medicine" (Dit Dar Jau) which can be obtained from any Chinese Medicine shop (located in most high streets). By dowsing the forearms both before and after a session of rigorous arm conditioning you will find that it not only aids recovery and the healing of bruises, but also subsides the pain. In time you will build a greater tolerance to the shock of impact to your skin, nerves and bones, to the point of absorbing punishing blows with no pain or bruises at all. The drill should be performed hard and fast in sharp and short powerful bursts, rather than prolonged sessions of weaker repetition.

Area of Contact

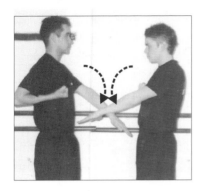 

1. Standing opposite each other in Goat Clamping Stance both partners (a) and (b) strike the inside of the lower forearm. Using an arc shape motion with their elbows locked straight.

2. Then using a Palm Up Arm position they simultaneously clash their outside lower forearms together. Using another arc shape motion.

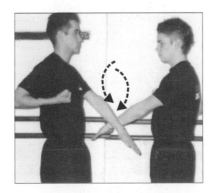

3. From there they complete the sequence by clashing the outside of their forearms using a Cultivating Arm position before repeating the drill on the other side

153

Arm Sensitivity

In conjunction to using arm toughening exercises it is equally important that you keep your arms balanced with the more subtle and softer sensitivity drill. This is a very simple exercise involving two persons with their forearms stretched out almost like having a double On Guard facing another double On Guard.

One practitioner must keep the eyes shut at all times while the other person takes an arm away as fast as possible in order to not telegraph ones movement. Upon feeling the sensation of this, the person with the eyes shut will spring forward with an immediate touch response as fast as possible usually to the chest region. By doing this drill with repetition you will find general reflexes and reactions can be improved.

Also do some switching variations, for instance moving the forearm so they are either both to the outside rather than both on the inside or one arm to the outside with the other to the inside and so on. You will find that this exercise will be helpful for the next stage of tactile hand/touch development known as Dan Chi Sau or Single Sticking Arm which can be found later on in this book.

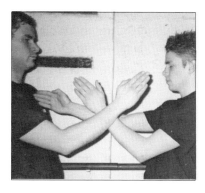

1. Facing each other with their arms touching together partner (a) quickly retracts his arm while partner (b) with his eyes closed responds on feeling by springing forwards immediately with a touch to the chest.

2. This time partner (a) takes away his right arm and (b) responds to the gap with a touch to the chest. Practice this drill at random varying the arm positions from the inside to the outside of the arms.

Fighting Applications

There are many variations of using Lin Sil Dai Dar - Simultaneous Attack and Defence, here are just a few examples of their practical application. The Dar could be translated as meaning "Hit" or "Strike" and does not specify any particular movement, so it could mean a punch, chop, palm, a kick or finger strike etc.

Tang Dar

Using a turning motion, angle the rear arm into a Tang Sau - Palm Up arm position while punching with the lead arm.

The counter attack can be used against a high to mid section hook, cross or straight punch.

Garn Dar

Using a turning motion, angle the rear arm into a Garn Sau - Cultivating Arm position while punching with the lead arm.

The counter attack can be used against a low to mid section hook or straight punch.

Lop Dar

Using a turning motion, angle the rear arm into a Lop Sau - Grabbing hand position while punching with the lead arm.

The counter attack can be used against a high, mid or low section cross or straight punch.

Gum Dar

Using a turning motion, angle the rear arm into a Gum Sau - Pinning Arm position while punching with the lead arm.

The counter attack can be used against a mid to low cross or straight punch.

Lan Dar

Using a turning motion, angle the rear arm into a Lan Sau - Barring Arm position while punching with the lead arm.

The counter attack can be used against a mid to low uppercut or straight punch.

Paak Sau

Using a turning motion, angle the rear arm into a Paak Sau - Slapping Hand position while punching with the lead arm.

The counter attack can be used against a high to mid section cross or straight punch.

Bong Dar

Using a turning motion, this time angle the lead arm into a Bong Sau - Wing Arm position while finger striking with rear arm.

The counter attack can be used against a mid to low cross or straight punch.

Here are some fighting applications using a Paak Sau - Slapping Hand entry to a Simultaneous Double Attack and Defence.

1. Partner (a) through a straight punch to the chin while partner (b) defends with a Paak Sau to bridge the gap.

2. Upon the next punch partner (b) counter attacks using a Lop Dar - Grabbing Arm (using a Chan Sau - Chop combined with Wang Ding Gerk - Thrusting Kick).

1. Partner (a) begins to launch a straight punch while partner (b) intercepts and dissolves it a Paak Sau to bridge the gap.

2. Partner (b) immediately sectors partner (a) with a Tang Dar - Palm up arm (using a Sau Do - Palm up chop combined with Tong Gerk - Stomp Kick).

PART 8
SINGLE STICKING ARM

Dan Chi Sau
Single Sticking Arm

This two man drill is designed to let the practitioner gain a feeling for sensitivity and reaction which will lead to the next step of Wing Chun known as Double Sticking Arms. To develop the certain energies required to perform the Single Sticking Arm it is necessary that it is learnt slowly in stages until the complete drill has been cultivated.

In order to do this it is essential to;
1) Make sure all hand movements are correct
2) Correct timing and tempo with a pause when in the neutral Palm Up Arm position.
3) Feeling the opponents movement upon execution and responding naturally rather than anticipating what you know will follow next.

There are numerous variations of the Sticking Arm drill but this is by far the most popular and once fully understood it will be easy to actually apply different movements to formulate your very own drill or combination.

The Single Sticking Arm consists of six actions excluding the change and is performed in a relaxed manner from the Goat Clamping Stance position. Correct repetition of Single Sticking Arm will ensure quickened reflexes due to the development of new muscle groups in conjunction to the memory concentration.

Single Sticking Arm (Preparation)

Part One

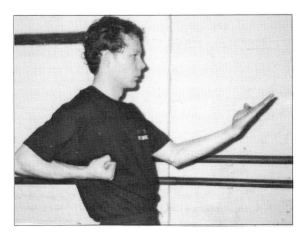

1. Tang Sau - Palm Up Arm: Hold the elbow at a finger and thumb distance from the chest with the palm facing upwards. Maintaining a forty five degree angle

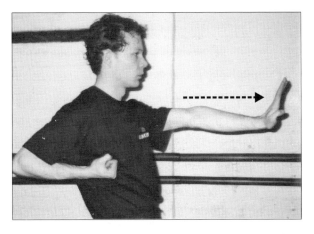

2. Jueng - Palm: Thrust out a palm strike at chest heart while turning the wrist as far as possible.

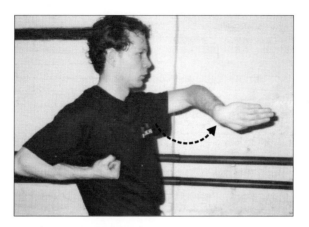

3. Bong Sau - Wing Arm: Lift the elbow and drop the wrist simultaneously with a corkscrew motion. Shoulders relaxed and fingers pointing forward

Part Two

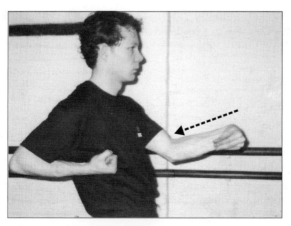

1. Fok Sau - Controlling Arm: Hold the elbow at a finger and thumb distance from the chest with the wrist bent as far as possible. Bunch all fingers together touching the thumb.

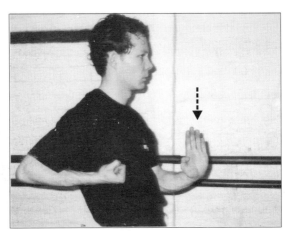

2. Wu Sau - Praying Arm: With a small semi circle moving downwards (not backwards) and the fingers pointing upwards to form a Praying Arm position.

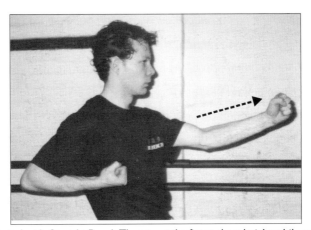

3. Noy Chung Choi - Inside Straight Punch: Thrust out the fist at chest height while retaining a small bend in the elbow.

166

Single Sticking Arm

Part One

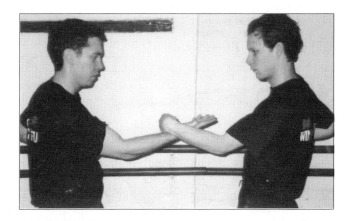

1. Partner (a) forms a Tang Sau position while partner (b) rests his Fok Sau around(a) wrist. (Neutral

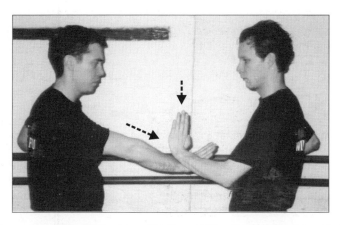

2. Partner (a) thrust out a Juerng to the chest of (b). Partner (b) on feeling responds with a Wu Sau.

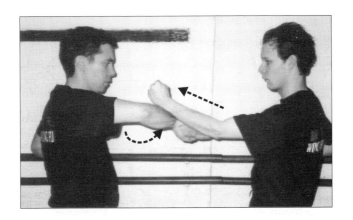

3. Partner (b) follows this with a Noy Chung Choi to the chest of (a). Partner (a) on feeling responds with a Bong Sau.

Part Two

1. The role is reversed so that partner (a) rests his Fok Sau on the Tang Sau of partner (b). (Neutral Position)

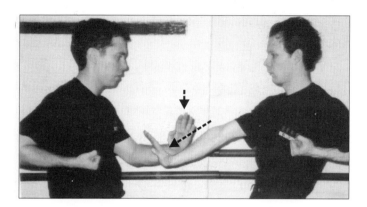

2. Partner (b) launches a Juerng to the chest and (a) reacts using a Wu Sau to block it.

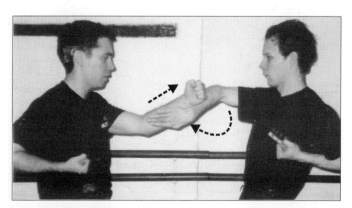

3. Partner (a) thrusts a Noy Chun Choi and (b) employs the Bong Sau to deflect it before returning to the neutral position to repeat the drill again.

PART 9
ADDITIONAL THEORY

Skill Refinement

In order to use Wing Chun with total effectiveness it requires plenty of enhancing skills and attributes. No single magic technique will work in a panicked situation, only a mixture of speed hand to eye, contact reflexes, evasive footwork etc; will aid the practitioner to succeed in violence.

Dexterity and co-ordination must not be overlooked as they all play a major role in the development of skill refinement. Before beginning a training session you should think about the area of skill that you want to improve so you can work on it, for example if you want faster punching then use a combination of light hand weights, interval sprinting and a stop watch to time yourself.

Maintenance of Skills

More than just repetition of techniques it is imperative that the practitioner repeats what they are learning in a correct way so as not to ingrain any bad habits into their practice.

Many people tend to forget their basics when they are concentrating on more advanced movements but this is in fact a step backwards in their development. Always try to find time to fit some kind of practice whenever possible and always remember to maintain the key basics. Too often people overwork themselves and thus reach a "burn out" stage through either injury or boredom and this is why it is better to build in stages. You have probably heard of the saying "repetition is the Mother of all techniques" and its true! Remember champions put up with all the tedious and repetitive aspects of their training (what ever it may be) and keep going where others give up. Winners never quit, quitters never win!

Bad Training Habits

One of the most important things with correcting training errors is the knowing of when you are practicing something wrong. But how do you realise what you are doing is wrong? "If you always did what you've always done, you will always get what you've always got"

Here are some tips on how to avoid common training mistakes;

1) Train consistently every week without gaps under a reputable source. Stopping and starting the learning process has a counter effect on positive results. "No practice, No progress"

2) "You heard but did you listen?" One of the main problems is not having the new information relayed to you clearly. You must listen to your Master very carefully.

3) Analyse what you are doing. Check the angles and every minor detail. Take a look how the others do it. Use the mirror to help correct positions both from front and side view.

4) Make notes whenever possible so you can record the areas you might forget later. Bring a note pad and pen to every training session.

5) Aim for actually understanding what you are doing. You need to cultivate a good "Working Knowledge" instead of just blindly going through the motions. Does it work for you?

6) Stay alert when practicing any skill enhancing drills. Doing them while you are too tired will develop sloppy techniques and it might effect your speed, timing and tempo permanently.

7) If you are too tired to practice skills that require lots of concentration then switch to stamina and endurance drills.

8) "Repetition is the Mother of all technique." Once you have the correct information relayed to you, you need to practice it over and over until it is absolutely ingrained into your body and mind.

9) Try not to overwork yourself when training. Your re-couperation is paramount to your success so always make sure you have ample rest periods so that your body can recover. Sometimes you may not feel like training because you are too tired from work, so take a power nap for an hour before training so you feel energised.

10) Training for 10-15 minutes a day is more beneficial then training for several hours once a week. Don't try to allocate too much time to practice (when starting out) as the chances of you sticking to it are quite rare. People often start out with all the good intentions but usually end up losing interest or sight of what they are doing due to overtraining before they are ready. So pace yourself. "The candle that burns the brightest lasts the least amount of time"

Reality Within Training

No single style can claim superiority. It is purely down to the individual and how much effort they put into their training. Wing Chun Kung Fu is a relatively modern system in comparison to other Kung Fu systems which date back to the Pre-Medieval times of China and contain vast amounts of bare hand and weapons training set patterns. Many of these styles have no real practical value in regards to self defence nowadays as so much has changed in the world (such as crime, social, technology etc;), where as Wing Chun remains highly functional and this is probably due to the lack of so many pre arranged forms and of course the no nonsense approach based on the concept of the Economy of motion (stressing logic and not wastage of physical movement).

In order to develop effective Martial Art skills you must practice with some zeal of reality rather than just going through the motions. It is all too easy to create a comfort zone through controlling the situation by using a weaker opponent or working on your favourite technique, drill or side.After all no one will attack you the way you want in a real fight as it all happens so fast. There are also many implications to consider (like multiple/armed attackers, environment, mental attitude) and only by pressure testing yourself through a combination of hard work/ correct practice/ conditioning/ impact practice and metal awareness will you get a feeling for reality. "What's the point in having a pocket full of knives if none of them cut"

Less is More

It is much better to have a small repertoire of well trained techniques rather than a huge collection of half baked ones. You are much more likely to respond effectively in a violent confrontation if you do this, because having too many could leave you scratching your head pondering over what movement would work best!

Bruce Lee was a great advocate of the less is more idea which is all about the Economy of Motion and conservation of physical energy. An ancient proverb he used a lot (and one of my favourites) sums this up perfectly "One technique well mastered is better than a thousand half learned".

Tang Sau Ng the founder of Wing Chun (or at least one of them!) could apparently repel any attack with his perfected Tang Sau / Palm Up or Spread Out Arm hence his nickname. This in itself is recorded proof that less is definitely more when it comes to fighting. It is true, knowledge is power and although this might seem a little confusing it is important to know plenty of varied techniques in order to size down and isolate the best ones that fit your build, situation and mentality.

Northern and Southern Influences

The contrast between the development of Northern and Southern Kung Fu systems vary greatly. In essence Northern boxing styles tend to use very low stances, long range arm strikes, high kicks and usually but not always some acrobatics. This is because in the Northern part of China there is plenty of room to move around, vast open spaces, mountains and rugged terrain. Also we have to take into account that weather wise it can get very cold. So the styles of North are considered very rigorous and physically demanding, probably out of necessity to keep warm and because they have the room to practice.

Where as if you look at the way Southern styles have evolved you will see how they employ more shallow stances, low kicks, and a larger range of hand techniques. This stems from the theory that the Southern Provinces of China have very hot weather coupled with over populated villages. Therefore we have to take into account the climate, social, cultural, historical, and nutritional differences and how they influenced the Chinese Martial Arts.

A few years ago it was suggested that Wing Chun originated in the North and was then bought to the South where the masters expanded upon it and added their own unique elements. In my opinion this rumour could be bonefide, as historical chronicles record that either the (or one of the) founders "Tang Sau Ng" traveled from the North Province and settled in the Southern area of Canton.

Hard and Soft

"Hard" styles from the North are classified as being "External" in origin meaning they use physical effort more predominantly. Some of the systems that encompass the "Hard" are Pai Hok Kuen (White Crane), Zui Jiu Kuen (Drunkards Boxing), Ying Jow Pai (Eagle claw) and Hou Kuen (Monkey Boxing) to name but a few. The key element of their training would involve high explosive kicks, very low crouching postures and also tumbling actions.

"Soft" styles are known for the Internal training methods and have become more blatant in the South. Hsing I (Iron Wire) and Bag Gua (Mind Shape), are two popular "Internal" styles out of a vast list. In fact there are literally hundreds of both "Hard/External/Northern" and "Soft/Internal/Southern" styles.

There are also cross over styles. For instance there is a "Northern Praying Mantis" and a "Southern Praying Mantis" system but they are uniquely different. On top of all this there are many, many "Family Systems" that have evolved over time. Sometimes it is confusing for people getting started to find a style that fits their mentality and physical ability as style has its own attributes.

Some might say that "Soft/Internal" methods are more sophisticated, where as the "Hard/External" techniques are less subtle. This is simply not true as they are all refined and all take extreme (physical & mental) effort to learn and perform. Although Wing Chun is a "Southern" style it incorporates both "Hard & Soft" training elements. This might be something to do with why it is so adaptable for smaller people!

Amazing Comparisons

You would be surprised at the similarities between Hard (Northern) and Soft (Southern) styles of Kung Fu. Although some are vastly different in terms of their initial appearance, closer study shows us that there are many parallels.

Take a look outside of Chinese Martial Arts and you'll see that all pugilistic systems especially the Japanese, Filipino, Indonesian, (and plenty of other Asian and Non-Asian) share the same training methods and techniques. Of course there are both dramatic and subtle differences with them, but still there is a cross over that is clear to see, Two common signs are; 1) using the opponents own power against themselves and 2) using the same energy sources such as the hips, elbows, wrists and breathing, etc; It is said that the Shaolin Temple is ancestor of all Martial Arts and this is probably true.

If you learn any system thoroughly, then you will find amazing comparisons in the training methods and applications of any system. Lots of people find that other styles "go hand in hand" with their own style. For instance Filipino Arnis de Mano has many similarities to Chinese Wing Chun and therefore they compliment each other perfectly.

Traditional and Modern

The method of traditional learning the "Chinese way" involves a lot self realisation or basically trial and error. Emphasis is placed on humility and respect towards the teacher and fellow classmates. The training is very slow, arduous and even painstaking. You will learn in "bite size" portions leaving you wondering if you will ever be taught anything new! Traditional Masters are almost unapproachable when you first start, and it is not wise to quiz them to much as this could cause offence. They might think you are questioning their authority.

True Masters come in all shapes and sizes leading you to believe that they might not know anything just because they don't fit your expectations but "Never judge a book by its cover". Some Masters might not be perfect role models either. But their technical knowledge might be brilliant. Communication can also be a problem; (This is a true story) Once upon a time there was a Master that killed eleven of his own disciples by accident. Being illiterate he could not explain the finer points of the techniques and therefore could only demonstrate them for real.

Modern ways of teaching are much more forthcoming in comparison to the traditional approach. The communication is more open and learning pace is much faster. Modern methods of training tend to utilise more training equipment. Less emphasis is placed on the various rituals associated with Traditional Kung Fu.

So which is better? I hear you say. Well, that depends on what you want. I have experienced both the Traditional and Modern teachings and I would have to say that they both have something to offer. There are "pearls of wisdom" to learn in each of them. If you have only known the Modern way how can you know what the Traditional way is like? And visa versa.

"One who is too insistent on his views, finds few can agree with him"

Finding a Teacher

Before you embark on joining a Wing Chun school you should do your homework. By this I mean go and read up on the subject as much as possible. If you don't have the funds to buy some books then you can order them for free from any library, in fact they will probably already have some titles on their shelves. Reading will give you a head start on knowing what type of Wing Chun club and teacher you want learn from. Scan the Internet, there is a wealth of knowledge to be found on all Martial Arts. Yet again if you don't have access to a computer at home then you can use one at your local library. Also look at any applicable articles in the various Martial Arts publications that appear at the newsagents every month. In most of the magazines you will find a classified section (usually in the back) which lists the different clubs up and down the country.

Now please don't misunderstand me. I say none of this to disappoint you. I only mention it to make you realise that "big does not mean better" in the world of Martial Arts. In other words just because a club is packed with eager students in uniforms or the Kwoon (training hall) is luxurious and well equipped, does not mean the instructor or the style is authentic. Some bogus teachers are absolute masters when it comes to promoting and advertising their schools.

Choosing a decent Sifu (teacher) to learn from is paramount to anyone seeking to train seriously. Only he or she will be able to "nit pick" the very finer points of the system, overlooked by many other teachers. A good teacher will also be able to guide the student through the various esoteric practices.

If you can not train directly with one because of distance or cost then see if you can learn from their representative (if they have any) that might be nearer to you. If you want learn from a pure source then be sure to check the linage of your instructor and the extent of their knowledge.

Wing Chun Today

The standard of Wing Chun Kung Fu around the world today is of a very high quality thanks to the pioneering work of the late Grandmaster Yip Man students. You can find authentic Wing Chun schools in every corner of the globe including some obscure countries.

Years ago there was a lot of internal bickering between rival organisations who argued about who was right and wrong in the methods they were teaching. This became known as the "Wing Chun Wars" and seemed to be very harmful to the promotion of the system as there were so many contradictions being written in various Martial Art publications. Potential students were being put off by all the confusing and negative comments from different teachers of the style.

A few years ago a very famous Hong Kong Master who was responsible for perhaps one of the largest (if not the largest) schools around world, was exposed for being fraudulent. He had been deceiving people without question for years by claiming he was a original closed door disciple of Grandmaster Yip Man and even cut out and pasted a photo of himself standing next to the seated Grandmaster Yip Man! Luckily most of the Wing Chun clubs in existence today have accepted their differences and seem to be a little more united now then in previous years.

PART 10
THE SYLLABUS

Rolling and Sticking Arms

Look or Poon Sau-Rolling Arms is the next important phase of Wing Chun after learning the Single Sticking Arm drill thoroughly. Rolling Arms lets the practitioner gain tactile sensitivity, dexterity and co-ordination needed to control an opponent. With the sensation of using the skin and nerves to send messages to the brain already been developed through the Single Sticking Arm, the Rolling Arms provides the practitioner with the basis or framework for Suerng Chi Sau-Double Sticking Arms.

Upon first appearance this exercise seems relatively simple, but there is however much involved. You must go through various levels of Bik Ging - Pressing Energy to enhance the feeling and strengthen your "bridge" or forearms. In the early stages you can expect the shoulders to ache considerably and there is much to remember in terms of correct alignment and positions. Exercises are repeated over and over till they become neurologically imprinted into the mind. Only then does the random "non fixed" or free sparring stage take place.

Chi Gerk - Sticking Leg is yet another extension to sensitivity awareness using the legs to respond to attacks with foot stops, knee deflections, kicks and evasive footwork. Although this type of training becomes more apparent once the practitioner has studied the following two forms.

Essentially we want to be able to fight at all ranges of combat and therefore Double Sticking Arms helps us to achieve this. Once you have honed all the hand combinations and footwork that are accompanied with tactile sensitivity and touch reflex, you are then ready to learn the 2nd hand form of Wing Chun.

Searching for the Bridge

With the groundwork covered on the 1ˢᵗ form Little Idea the practitioners, next hand form to learn is the Chum Kiu - Searching for the Bridge.

This is a collection of movements that emphasise the defensive Wing and Barring Arm blocks it also contains elbows, uppercuts, kicks & footwork. The focus with the Searching for the Bridge form is to build Juen Ging -Turning Energy in the hips and gain total mobility through the practice of evasive footwork patterns.

Only when the practitioner has thoroughly digested the entire form can he / she begin to practice the practical fighting applications and apply them into their Double Sticking Arm practice.

116 Wooden Dummy Movements

The Mook Yan Jong-Wooden Dummy consists of a trunk or log either mounted on a frame, platform or traditionally embedded into the ground. The wooden pillar has two upper arms one on top of another pointing outwards, one mid section arm pointing forwards and on the lower portion a "leg" like structure protruding outwards.There are many various models of Wooden Dummy to be found in different styles of Kung Fu (some Wooden Dummies have a multitude of arms & legs!). The Wooden Dummy enables the student to practice when no training partners are available.

Grandmaster Yip Man originally condensed the form to only 108 movements, but then later revised it to 116 movements. The last few motions are repeated to underline their importance.

The focus on the form is the alignment of simultaneous hand & footwork positions combined to produce trapping or immobilisation effect. As before the practitioner must integrate the fighting applications soundly into the Double Sticking Arms exercise.

Darting Fingers

The last hand form of the Wing Chun system (before the introduction of the weapons forms) is Biu Jee - Darting Fingers. It is regarded as a some what "sacred" set of movements because of its use of deadly finger strikes (or Darts). Special blocking sequences, chops, elbows and energy breathing are all practiced fully.

The techniques of the form stress the use of attacking the vital areas and pressure points. The practical fighting applications should only be used in extreme circumstances in terms of a real life confrontation.

The last section of the form contains some unusual dipping or bending motions combined with large vigorous circles with the arms. This is meant to represent the freedom of reaching that stage of training. And therefore the practitioner has no bounds!

Six and Half Point Pole

The Lok Dim Gwan Boon - Six and a half Point Pole has only a very short set of movements in comparison to the other forms, but the fighting applications however are numerous.

The pole is 8 ft long and sometimes tapered at either one or both ends. It is said to have originated from the concept of a barge pole being used as a staff by the founders of the "Red Boat Opera Troupe".

The short sequence of movements, contain some old Shaolin stances such as the Horse, Cat, Dragon etc; The key focus is on developing "Chi/Qi" or energy in the end of the stick. Chi Gwan - Sticking Pole is a two man drill to build the smooth sticking motions needed for effective attack & counterattack techniques.

Butterfly Knives

This is the very last stage of training in the Wing Chun Kung Fu syllabus. In the old days they did have guns but they were not readily available so therefore people were forced to use Knives and Swords to protect themselves.

The Baat Jam Dau - Eight Slash Knives form uses two "meat cleaver" like knives (not to be confused with the Balisong - Filipino Butterfly Knife) to perform a sequence of motions. They can be thought of as an extension of ones arms and used to strengthen the wrists. There are plenty of two man drills and fighting applications that can be used against the pole.

Aside from this the Eight Slash Butterfly Knives should be learned to complete and preserve the tradition of Wing Chun Kung Fu.

Afterword

When I first started out learning and researching Wing Chun, I was lead to believe that it was simple. Nothing could have been further from the truth though! It is in fact a very complicated style to learn. The movements you so often see in books, magazines and on videos look relatively easy. That is until you learn how to do them correctly. All is not how it appears! The case of "Monkey see, monkey do" can not and must not apply to Wing Chun.

Basically it's different for everyone, as we are not "carbon copies". People differ in height, weight, intelligence etc; So they would all have differences about their Wing Chun such as; Angles of arm or leg positions or application etc; Grand Master Yip Man is noted to have taught students based on their backgrounds and they usually could be categorised into three types; 1)"Hot headed" teenagers and young adults who might need it if they got into gang fights 2) Professional people like cooks, builders, etc; who would use it more for a hobby 3) Doctors, Lawyers, and people of high intelligence capacity who practiced it for self protection and perfection of character. All of these types of people would have developed individual traits in relation to the way they performed their Wing Chun. You can see by this how some schools have differences between the vast and subtle.

From my own personal account, I had been training in Wing Chun for eleven years with a few different teachers. I had learned many of the forms, drills and applications only to be told that what I had been learning was entirely wrong! (This coming from a Hong Kong Master with direct lineage in the system was with out doubt the concise truth). And If I wanted to learn properly I would have to forget all the previous stuff and start all over again. This would be enough to put most people off. But some how I managed to "muster up" the will power to begin again.

The knowledge I had gained previously was, in fact, a major headache to me as I had developed some pretty indelible training habits. After much persistence I realised that what I was learning was quite different then before, even though it looked so similar. And above all the training was much, much harder! If you are learning Wing Chun or in fact any other Martial Art and your gushing with sweat through effort then you should seriously consider changing schools.

So why bother? Why the hell put yourself through the physical and physiological punishment? Because quite simply its DIFFICULT! Life is all about enduring struggle to attain the ultimate reality. Through the study of Martial skills we get a feeling of euphoria and a sense of achievement. It teaches you Life skills or more specifically how to accomplish and magnetise anything you want.

A great example of this would be my former teacher who, as a native of Hong Kong can speak several languages. Aside from his native Cantonese he can speak the national language of Mandarin Chinese, English, French, German, Italian, and Spanish fluently (and they were only the ones I knew about!!!) He was very modest I found these out gradually over the years. Someone would travel from say Germany to train with him and he would conduct, their entire lesson in German or what ever language they spoke. On top of this other "quiet" accomplishments that "unravelled" would make him an expert business man, golfing enthusiast, distance swimmer, "Core don bleu" Chef, skiing connoisseur, marksman, artist and much more. So he has learned how to become a scholar in life through the practice of Wing Chun a style he has practiced for over fifty years and never changed, diluted or deviated from.
"The purpose of life is a life of purpose"

Martial art training can benefit you beyond your wildest dreams if you are prepared to sacrifice yourself to hard work. You have to see past the physical "cover". It is not just about fighting.

I hope you enjoyed reading "Wing Chun Kung Fu a Southern Chinese Boxing system" as I mentioned earlier this was only meant to be a guide to compliment your own training regardless of what style you practice. In my next book "Sticking Arms sensitivity drills and Explosive Fighting applications" I will be taking a detailed look at the various Poon / Lok / Suerng Chi Sau training methods and applications. Variations of "Sticking Arms" from styles other than Wing Chun Kung Fu will be analysed to show their comparisons. Also I will include the entire 2nd form of Wing Chun "Chum Kiu" or Searching for the Bridge. The book will cover all the key footwork, elbows and kicking requirements.

Glossary of Terms

Arc Structure - One of the key theories of Wing Chun based on the idea of strength being gained from the triangular shape.

Arm Conditioning - Toughening the forearms through the repetition of striking various surfaces.

Arm Sensitivity - The cultivation of sensitivity in the skin, tissue and nerves of the arms for heightened tactile awareness.

Arnis de Mano / Kali / Escrima - A Filipino Warrior Fighting Art employing the use of single & double rattan canes, swords, knives & empty hand techniques

Baat Gwa Juerng / Ba Gua Zhang (Mandarin) - "Eight trigrams Palm" one of the major internal styles of Chinese boxing

Baat Jam Dau - Eight slash knives (advanced weapons form of Wing Chun Kung Fu involving two butterfly knives)

Bai Hok Kuen / Pai Hok Quan (Mandarin) - White crane boxing a northern Kung Fu system that utilises the movements of crane involving high kicking attacks, pounding wing like strikes and actions

Bai Jong - On guard or assume post

Bik Ging - Pressing energy

Biu Jee - Darting fingers (3rd hand form of Wing Chun Kung Fu)

Bong Sau - Wing arm

Chang Kuen / Chang Quan (Mandarin) - Long fist a northern Kung Fu style which comprises of low postures, slapping kicks and arc like fist & forearm attacks

Chan Sau - Chopping arm

Centreline Theory - An imaginary line going through the centre of the body and covering the all the major targets.

Chi Gerk - Sticking legs

Chi Gwan - Sticking Poles

Chi Sau - Sticking arms (the practice of arm sensitivity drills)

Chin Na - An old spelling abbreviation (see Kum na)

Choi - Punch

Chuen Ging - Inch force

Chung Choi- Straight punch

Chum Kiu - Searching for the bridge (2nd hand form of Wing Chun Kung Fu)

Dai Juerng- Low or sleeping palm

Dan Chi Sau - Single sticking arm (one arm sensitivity drills}

Dar - Hit or strike

Ding Gerk - Nailing kick

Dit Dar Jow / Teet Ta Chau (Mandarin) - A powerful Chinese liniment used to alleviate pain and heal bruises.

Economy of Motion - The concept of using the most efficient response or counterattack

Faatshan/Foshan (Mandarin) -The southern Chinese district of Canton (Guangdong) and birthplace of Wing Chun Kung Fu.

Fook Sau - Controlling arm

Garn Sau - Cultivating arm

Gat Sau - Arm toughening drill (see Arm conditioning or Sarm sing)

Gerk - Kick

Ging - A term used to describe power, energy or force.

Golden Targets - The vital areas of attack & defence

Grandmaster - A Master of the highest eminence.

Gum Gok Ging - Sensitivity & reaction energy

Gum Sau - Pressing or pinning arm

Gung Fu / Gong Fu (Mandarin) - An expression used to describe the attainment of skill through hard work.

Gung Lik - The building of internal & external energy through prolonged training.

Hand Conditioning - The toughening of ones hands through repetitive striking on bags filled with gravel to develop (see wall bag)

Hay Gung / Qi Gong (Mandarin) - Vital breathing energy cultivation exercises

Hsing I Kuen / Xing Yi Quan (Mandarin) - "Mind Form Boxing" one of the major internal styles of Chinese boxing

Hou Kuen / Tai Shing Men - A northern Chinese boxing system based around the characteristics of a monkey, incorporating intricate movements such as crouching, leaping and tumbling with deadly fighting techniques.

Huen Sau - Circling or rotating hand

Jeet Kune Do - "Way of the intercepting fist" a collection personal fighting ideas by Bruce Lee (see Jun Fan Gung Fu)

Joon Sien - A term used to describe the centreline

Jow Sau - Clawing arm

Juen Ma - Turning stance

Jull Ma - Running horse

Juerng - Palm

Jum Sau - Jerking arm

Jun Fan Gung Fu - "Small Phoenix" a modernised version of Wing Chun devised and named after the late Martial Artist, actor and founder of Jeet Kune Do Bruce Lee

Jui Kuen / Jui Quan (Mandarin) - Drunken boxing a complicated northern Kung Fu system involving deceiving movements, giving the appearance of being drunk while employing strikes & blocks

Jyeh Lik - Borrowing power

Kau Sau - Scooping or detaining arm

Kuen / Quan (Mandarin) - Fist, style or boxing

Kum Na / Qin Na (Mandarin) - Seizing & controlling techniques

Kung Fu - The westernised pronunciation for the Cantonese term of Gung Fu or Chinese term of Gong Fu

Kwoon - Training hall or Gymnasium

Lan Sau - Barring or Folding arm

Lau Gar Kuen / Liu Jia Quan (Mandarin) - Lau family style one of the five major "family" systems of southern Chinese Kung Fu

Lien Wan Choi - Centre Punching (Rapid concessive punches)

Lin Sil Dai Dar - Simultaneous attack & defence (see simultaneous attack & defence)

Lok Dim Boon Gwan - Six & a half point pole (advanced weapon form of Wing Chun Kung Fu involving an eight foot pole)

Lok Ma - A term used to describe the Wing Chun stance (see Yee jee kum yueng ma)

Lok Sau - Rolling arms (a double sticking arm exercise)

Lop Sau - Grabbing arm

Ma - Stance or posture

Mai Jan - Immovable elbow

Man Sau - Asking or begging arm

Mook Yan Jong - Wooden dummy a training apparatus used to practice footwork & hand techniques, consisting of a large wooden stake with three wooden arms & one leg, usually supported on a frame, floor platform, wall or traditionally buried into the ground

Mook Yan Jong Yat Saap Lok - 116 movements of the wooden dummy (training form of Wing Chun Kung Fu see above)

Ng Mui / Wu Mei (Mandarin) - Buddhist nun from the 17th century and one of the "Five elders" from the Shaolin Temple & legendary founder of the Wing Chun Kung Fu

Ngoi Chung Choi - Outside straight punch

Ngoi Lop - Outside grab

Ngoi Paak - Outside slap

Ngon Ging - Eye focusing energy

Noy Chung Choi - Inside straight punch

Noy Lop - Inside grab

Noy Paak - Inside slap

Paak Sau - Slapping arm

Pencak Silat - A deadly Indonesian Warrior fighting art with similarities to northern Chinese boxing styles

Poon Sau - Rolling arms another abbreviation for a two man exercise involving sensitivity (see Lok sau and Chi sau)

Sarm Sing - "Three star" an expression used to describe three major areas of conditioning ones arms

Sau - Arm or hand

Sau Do - Palm up chop

Sifu / Shifu (Mandarin) - Polite form of address meaning teacher, master or esquire (two syllables lit. Teacher/Father)

Si Gung / Shi Gong (Mandarin) - Grand teacher / Master (see Grandmaster)

Sil Lum / Shaolin (Mandarin) - The monasteries in China where all Martial Arts can be traced to

Simultaneous Attack & Defence - Combining blocking and striking gestures to gain the advantage of your opponents

Six Gates of Attack - The principle of using visualisation to divide the body into six separate sections for attack & defence purposes

Suerng - Double

Suerng Chi Sau - Double sticking arms

Sui Nim Tau - Little idea (1st hand form of Wing Chun Kung Fu)

Tang Sau - Palm up or spread out arm

Tang Sau Ng - One of the founders of Wing Chun Kung Fu nicknamed "Tang sau" because peerless palm up arm techniques

Teet Sa Choi - Iron palm (see Hand conditioning)

Teet Sau Juerng - Iron palm (see Hand conditioning)

Tok Sau - Lifting hand

Tong Gerk - Stomp Kick

Tong Long Kuen / Tang Lang Quan (Mandarin) - Praying mantis boxing a type of Kung Fu with two distinct northern & southern styles incorporating the clawing & gouging hand movements and elusive footwork of a praying mantis

Tut Sau - Freeing or breakout arm

Ving Tsun Kuen - A westernised spelling for Wing Chun devised by the late Grandmaster Yip Man (see Wing Chun Kuen)

Wang Juerng - Side palm

Wang Ding Gerk - Side Nailing Kick

Wang Gerk - Side Kick

Wall Bag - A canvas bag which can be filled with sand, soya beans, gravel, pebbles or metal ballbearings used for toughening the hands and developing "inch force" (see hand conditioning)

Wing Chun Kuen / Yong Chun Quan (Mandarin) - Always spring boxing a southern Chinese Kung Fu system involving combined attack & defence movements, low kicks, and "sticking techniques"

Wing Tsun - A spelling term used describe a modernised version of Wing Chun

Wu Dip Dau - Double butterfly knives (see Baat jam dau)

Yau - Springiness or elasticity

Yip Man - The late Grandmaster of Wing Chun Kung Fu who was instrumental in introducing the system from its birthplace of Faatshan Canton to the people of Hong Kong between the 1950s & 1970s

Yim Wing Chun - An orphan girl disciple nicknamed "a new hope for the future" by the fabled originator (see Ng Mui)

Yum / Yuerng / Yin / Yang (Mandarin) - A term used to describe the direct opposites upon which life and the science of the universe rely such as; darkness/lightness, negative/positive, moon/sun, left/right, feminine/masculine, destruction/construction etc;

Ying Jow Pai / Yin Zhao Pai (Mandarin) - Eagle claw boxing a northern Kung Fu system based around the motions of an eagle combining low crouching postures, leaping, aerial kicking with clawing & ripping hand attacks